Indispensable

How to Become
the Company That
Your Customers
Can't Live Without

Joe Calloway

WILEY

John Wiley & Sons, Inc.

Published by John Wiley & Sons, Inc., Hoboken, New Jersey.
Published simultaneously in Canada.

For general information on our other products and services please contact our Customer
Care Department within the United States at (800) 762-2974, outside the United States
at (317) 572-3993 or fax (317) 572-4002.

Wiley also publishes its books in a variety of electronic formats. Some content that
appears in print may not be available in electronic books. For more information about
Wiley products, visit our web site at www.wiley.com.

Library of Congress Cataloging-in-Publication Data:
Calloway, Joe.
    Indispensable: how to become the company that your customers can't live
without / Joe Calloway.
        p.   cm.
    ISBN 0-471-70308-7 (cloth)
    1. Customer loyalty.   2. Customer loyalty—Case studies.   I. Title.
    HF5415.525.C35 2005
    658.8'343—dc22
                                                            2004028133

Printed in the United States of America.
10 9 8 7 6 5 4 3 2 1

For Annette
The one I can't live without.

Acknowledgments

Thanks to Coke Sams, whose title idea was much better than mine; Michelle Joyce, whose subtitle idea was *infinitely* better than mine; and especially to Ellen Bush for being a fabulous rough draft editor.

Contents

Preface

From the television viewer who would always tape rather than miss a single episode of HBO's *Sex and The City,* to the corporate buyer who will choose a trusted vendor over a lower priced competitor, there are customers who consider certain products or companies indispensable. It's the mother lode . . . the jackpot . . . the Holy Grail of business: loyal customers who want to do business with you, and only you when buying your product or service.

Think of a company that you wouldn't want to live without. We all have at least one. It might be your overnight shipping provider, an auto repair shop, or the Internet company that provides your office supplies. What's their secret to winning your business and continuing loyalty? How do they do it? And, most important, what are they doing that you should be doing with your own customers?

Indispensable companies are the ones that win the bid even though a competitor came in with a lower price. They are the ones we'll drive out of our way to patronize even though we could buy the same product at a more convenient location. And they are most often the companies that have created the most profitable relationships with customers.

So how do you become indispensable? What's the secret to becoming the company that your customers can't live without? That's what this book is about. It's a study of the factors that make a company a complete, total, absolute necessity to its customers. Identifying the factors is actually pretty easy. Implementation and execution tend to be a bit tougher. As the old saying goes, "Ideas are funny things. They don't work unless we do."

Becoming indispensable means becoming the default choice. When a customer needs what you sell, she chooses you automatically, almost without thought. You become a habit. The idea is to be a customer magnet, pulling business past your competition and right into your door, or catalog, or web site.

Indispensable companies have a clear sense of focus on where they "fit" in the grand scheme of the marketplace. It begins with a few age old, vitally important questions:

- What do we do best?
- What do we love to do?
- What do our customers value?
- Where do those three factors intersect?

That magic intersection is where companies begin to differentiate in a significant way from their competition.

Most people are interested in practical application rather than theory, so this book is heavy on real-world examples. The case studies of indispensable companies range from a check printer in a shrinking market that is reinventing itself through a remarkable collaborative process with customers; a hotel chain that locks in customer loyalty with a unique and compelling experience; a restaurant whose customers line up around the block to partake of a magic blend of pancakes and personality; a seminar company that provides continuing education to attorneys—delivered with a "concierge" philosophy; a bank that built, from scratch, a model of how to transcend commodity in the highly competitive financial services industry; and a sales consultant/trainer/speaker/ writer who has created raving fans by creating value, then giving it away.

While every company I studied achieved success in its own unique way, there were five factors that they all had in common. I call these factors the *Five Drivers:*

1. Create and sustain momentum.
2. Develop habitual dependability.
3. Continuous connection.
4. Big picture outcome.
5. Engage, enchant, and enthrall.

Along with the Five Drivers, I discovered that indispensable companies have all embraced some key ideas that pretty much make up the way they look at the world. They include continuously asking, "Why not?" and challenging convention . . . getting back *inside* the box to be sure that you've mastered the basics before you bet the ranch on innovation . . . partnering in ways that access previously untapped sources of business . . . understanding that traditional approaches to selling are dead . . . that whatever happens is normal and that mental toughness, not positive thinking, is what creates opportunity in any situation, and that the Internet didn't change anything in terms of what truly matters in business.

One point that is made throughout the book is that becoming indispensable requires creativity. There is no template for success, nor is there a fill-in-the-blanks 10-step guide or a color-by-numbers picture-painting approach to success. It's not that easy. You have to figure it out. Take the incredibly powerful strategy of creating community among your customers. Creating community is a strategy that has been used to great advantage by indispensable entities ranging from Apple's iPod, to the rock band Los Lobos. Becoming the common bond among a group of customers takes you to a whole new level of prominence, and it's a lesson that any business can put to good use. It requires, however, the creative vision to look at how other companies have tapped the powerful marketing force of creating community and figuring out your version of it. This isn't about copying what another company has done. It's about letting examples of innovation in a wide range of businesses serve as a catalyst for your own imagination.

Perhaps the most striking lesson I learned in researching indispensable companies is that they have a firm grasp on some seemingly obvious but often overlooked factors in business. Some of these get into "Duh!" territory, like the incredible power of a first impression, or telling customers the truth, or that doing your job and delivering what the customer is paying for does NOT equal exceeding anybody's expectations.

It's often been said that success comes from being at the right place at the right time, and I wholeheartedly agree. In fact, indispensable companies make it an integral part of their strategy to be at the right place at the right time as often as possible. It's much more than physical location or having a great web site. Being accessible to customers and giving them what they want, the way they want it, when they want it is a matter of design, not luck. It's also a matter of every employee having a constant, unwavering focus on the customer.

Of the Five Drivers, perhaps the most powerful is the idea of Big Picture Outcome. It's so important that it gets its own chapter in the book. Mediocre companies are transaction focused. Indispensable companies, and everyone in them, are outcome focused—creating outcomes for their customers. It's a matter of every employee being fully present in the sense of total engagement far beyond the immediate delivery of a product or service.

Big Picture Outcome requires that you embrace a customer-centric philosophy that drives everything you do.

You may have wondered why every company, even the really bad ones, seem to be able to come up with a gloriously written mission statement. I can't think of a company that isn't perfect on paper. Their mission and vision statements read like a customer's dream. So where's the disconnect? Why is it that so many well-intentioned companies can't consistently deliver quality products, service, and experiences? All too often, it's a simple case of intention without execution. Old saying: Vision without execution is an hallucination. Here's the key: repeatable process. This is the missing link between intention and reality. With a repeatable process, you can achieve the brand strength that comes only from consistency.

One chapter is devoted to Twenty-Eight Indispensable Ideas. Consider it a brain-storming session from which you take away ideas that you can immediately apply. From how Target competes successfully against lower priced competitors to how NASCAR makes it personal to Harrah's Casinos understanding the one thing that their customers really want—these are all lessons that you can adapt to your own business to create success.

In this book, you're going to get ideas on how to become indispensable from companies that you might think have little in common with your business. The truth is that the most powerful lesson for your company may very well be found in the strategies that Oprah Winfrey used to build an empire, or that W Hotels used to innovate their way to success in the hospitality business.

Keep an open mind. When you most need the lesson, the teacher will appear. If you need lessons in how to become the company that your customers can't live without, this book will prove to be a good teacher.

1

The Default Choice

Quick—Give Me a Name

If you were to list categories and say to me, "Quick, give me a name!" it would go something like this:

Advertising agency: Engel Creative—They're the only ad agency I've used for 20 years.

Computer services: Bytes of Knowledge—My computer crashes. They fix it. Period.

Martini: Any martini made by Stephanie at Mirror—She is the Martini Goddess.

Pen: Flair—My workhorse writing instrument. I can't quit 'em.

Breakfast: The Pancake Pantry. Go there and you'll understand.

Clothes: Saks Fifth Avenue. I buy clothes at many places, but if I could choose only one place, I'd take the men's store at Saks Fifth Avenue.

Newspaper: The *New York Times*—I sometimes read three or four newspapers a day. If I could read only one, this would be it.

You get the idea. In each of those product categories, I have a default choice. These companies have become indispensable to me. I can't live without them. Well, okay, that's an exaggeration. I can live without them, I suppose, but I don't want to.

I'm always looking for lessons that I can use. That's the whole purpose of this book. To give you lessons you can use to make your business indispensable to your customers. There are many threads of excellence that the companies in this book have in common. One is that each company has established dominance in one area. They each have their turf, and you know what it is. There's no confusion about what they're good at. By the way, in the interest of full disclosure, Stephanie the Martini Goddess is the bartender at Mirror, where I'm a partner. If she ever goes to work at another bar, I'll probably follow her, have a martini there, then go back to my own restaurant for dinner. She's that good. And make no mistake about it, it's not really the martini. It's Stephanie. Her customers like her martinis, but they love her. That's not just my opinion, either. The *Nashville Scene's* 2004 "Best of Nashville" readers' poll voted Stephanie second place in the "Best Bartender" category. Second? Personally, I think she was robbed.

Go through your own personal list of "Quick, give me a name!" choices in a variety of product or service categories, then look for threads. What do they all have in common? What do they do that you should be doing? What's your version of the particular strength or advantage that they have developed? This, by the way, is where most people get stuck. They don't have the creative vision required to look at a business totally different from theirs and see what the transferable lessons are. Pity. They lose.

That's why every business but one in any given category is a follower. In their quest for the magic template that they can simply lay on top of their company, people benchmark the best companies in their industry, then try to copy them. This strategy, by definition, means that you will always be an imitator, a follower, and second place at best. One way to help spark innovative ideas is to look outside your own business and see what's working for companies with which, on the face of it, you appear to have nothing in common.

Best Pizza on the Block

I once saw a cartoon of three pizza restaurants all lined up on the same street. One had a massive sign out front that screamed "Best Pizza in the State." The next had a somewhat smaller sign that proclaimed "Best Pizza in the City." The third was the only one that had a line of waiting customers that stretched outside and down the sidewalk. It had the smallest sign of all, which read "Best Pizza on the Block." Get it? The idea is that you stake out your turf and master it.

For you, your turf may be a product category or an area of expertise. The goal is to become that default choice in the minds of your customers. You want your customers to stop thinking, and act from an almost instinctive motivation. You want to become ingrained into your customers' brains in a way that causes tunnel vision through which they see only you. You want to become the default choice.

Price Plummets in Importance

One of the greatest advantages achieved by attaining indispensable status is that price plummets in importance as a factor in the decision-making process. Looking at my list of default choices, I know that when I have a new marketing program to launch, I have total and complete tunnel vision. I call Todd Engel at Engel Creative and turn the job over to him. Todd works his magic, and I pay the bill. I can't remember the last time that price was a consideration. I may ask what his ballpark estimate is on a project, but it's purely for informational purposes, not really as part of the decision. If he thinks it's worth the money, I say go.

I recently referred a colleague to Todd for some marketing work. My friend called and said that he had gotten an estimate from Todd, and wanted to know if I thought Todd's fees were in line with his competition. I told him that I had no idea. What I did know was that I loved Todd's work, and I loved working with his company. Whatever they charge, I pay. I don't shop it around. He's indispensable.

The same goes for Bytes of Knowledge. My computers go down or develop a mysterious malfunction and I go into default mode. I call Bytes of Knowledge, someone comes over and fixes the problem, then they send me a bill and I pay it. I know for a fact that others charge less. This is irrelevant to me. I am typical of today's customer who places a high value on dependability and consistency of performance. I'm looking for the sure thing. I don't have the time, patience, or money to waste on any company that can't get it right the first time.

Master of One

What Engel Creative, Bytes of Knowledge, and most other indispensable companies have in common is that they are masters of one thing. They know their turf; that's what they focus on; and to their customers they have become a category of one. The age-old, time-tested approach to success through focus requires answering three basic questions:

1. What do we do *best*?
2. What do we *love* to do?
3. What do our customers *value*?

How do those three factors match up? Where do they intersect?

A classic mistake in business is to go after more customers by expanding your product or service offerings too far. This can be a great move, but it's a little like "thinking outside the box." Sometimes I have to advise my clients that before they start to think outside the box, they'd better take care of what's inside the box. In other words, innovation is great, but don't spend money, time, and energy on innovation if you haven't first mastered the basics.

The same goes for diversification. For most companies, the answer to developing new business isn't to add products or services, but to master the product or service you already offer. Getting better at your core offering will usually get you a much greater return in new customers and increased business with existing customers than the same efforts put into diversification would bring. Look at whatever you do and get better at it. Then get better again. And, if it makes sense to add products and services to your business, beware of the almost inescapable trap of letting quality slip. "Hey, you know what else we could do?" were all too often a failed company's famous last words.

This is not to say in any way that you should stop changing, innovating, or improving. On the contrary, you will never be the master of anything unless you are willing to constantly move forward. Becoming really good at one thing does not mean doing it exactly the same way year after year. The marketplace will leave you behind if you don't always strive to do it better on a continuing basis.

Do You Love It?

After answering the question "What do we do best?" move on to "What do we love to do?" The answer may surprise you. Many companies find their breakthrough to becoming indispensable through a realignment of what they love to do with what they are good at doing. That can sometimes mean some painful letting go of what's bringing in revenue, but not bringing in personal satisfaction. It's a long-term strategy; continuing to do what you don't love will ultimately result in failure on some level.

If it's not fun, don't do it. This idea will crawl all over those who like to see themselves as pragmatists, not interested in business as a "party," but strictly as a revenue creating endeavor. Hey, I'm about 50 of the most pragmatic people you'll ever meet, all rolled into one. But there's nothing pragmatic or practical or effective about trying to force the process of doing work you don't enjoy. It's ineffective and unhealthy. In the short term, you might make some money doing something that makes you miserable.

But today's market demands that you create compelling experiences for customers. You can't do that with people whose hearts aren't in it. It simply doesn't happen. You know that from your own experience as a customer. You can only fake enthusiasm and commitment for so long, then the game is up and you'll be busted by customers who see through the charade.

Being Good at It and Loving It Aren't Enough

It's that third question that makes the final determination of where your business should go. What do our customers value?

Here's where the rubber meets the road. You can be great at something you absolutely adore doing, but if nobody is willing to pay you for it, what you've got is a hobby, not a business. That's the problem with the inspirational but sometimes misguided notion of "Do what you love. The money will follow." Ditto for "Follow your bliss." Hey, nobody loves bliss more than me. I'm totally in favor of bliss and partake of it as often as possible. But what's up for discussion here is business. From my own experience, I can testify that just because I love to do it that doesn't mean anybody loves for me to do it to the point that they'll pay me for it. I'm one of those people who find creative satisfaction in my work, but it's not what I love most in the world. That would be my wife Annette and our daughter Jess. And my friends, family, and my life away from work. But what I have done is find work that I enjoy, that I am good at, that matches up with market demand. Voila. That's what you call a viable business. Now all I have to do is keep getting better at it.

Customer Magnet

I got off the plane in Cincinnati wanting a particular product. As I walked through the airport I passed first one, then another, and yet a few more businesses that sold this product. They all offered a good version of the product at a reasonable, competitive price. I continued walking. When I got to the center section of the terminal I turned and walked out of my way, taking a detour to get to the place I was looking for. When I found it, I stood in line and waited until I moved my way up to the counter, placed my order, and cheerfully paid about 300 percent more for the product than I would have at any of the other places I had passed.

Of course you know where I was—Starbucks. Starbucks has become exactly what you want your business to become—a customer magnet. The Starbucks brand quite literally pulls customers past its competitors and into its doors for coffee and everything else they sell. Why do half the business magazines on the newsstand at any given time seem to have a Starbucks story on the cover? Because they've done it. They've pulled it off. To their customers, they have become indispensable.

Starbucks has found that magic intersection of what they love to do, what they do best, and what their customers value. They've cracked the code. They know their turf. It's coffee and, more important, the entire experience surrounding the coffee. To their customers, Starbucks is famous.

Being Famous

Being the default choice and becoming indispensable to your customers means, ultimately, being famous. Not to everyone. Just to your customers and potential customers. Rarely is this kind of marketplace fame achieved by doing anything particularly exotic. It's achieved by doing something that may be considered quite ordinary, but doing it extraordinarily well.

I discovered the most wonderful perspective on being famous in a poem by the fabulous writer Naomi Shihab Nye. It's about being famous in a sense that you may never have considered. By taking the concept of being famous and bringing it down to the perspective of who you serve and how well you perform, we can gain a valuable insight into what really matters most. I offer it to you as a wonderful approach to doing business, and I encourage you to buy every book she's ever written. A good place to start is *Words Under the Words: Selected Poems*. Read Naomi's work and she'll likely become as indispensable to you as she has to me.

Famous

The river is famous to the fish.
The loud voice is famous to silence,
which knew it would inherit the earth before anybody said so.
The cat sleeping on the fence is famous to the birds watching him from the birdhouse.
The tear is famous, briefly, to the cheek.
The idea you carry close to your bosom is famous to
your bosom.
The boot is famous to the earth,
more famous than the dress shoe,
which is famous only to floors.
The bent photograph is famous to the one who carries it and
not at all famous to the one who is pictured.
I want to be famous to shuffling men who smile while
crossing streets,
sticky children in grocery lines,
famous as the one who smiled back.
I want to be famous in the way a pulley is famous,
or a buttonhole, not because it did anything spectacular,
but because it never forgot what it could do.

Read those last lines one more time, because they get to the
heart of what becoming indispensable is all about:

I want to be famous in the way a pulley is famous,
or a buttonhole, not because it did anything spectacular,
but because it never forgot what it could do.

That's it! Be famous because you never forget what you can do.
Thank you, Naomi, for that simple and profound wisdom.

2

The Five Drivers

Monotonous Success

When I talk with the leaders of extraordinarily successful companies with a loyal customer following, they all say pretty much the same thing. It's become very predictable, almost monotonous. And, somewhat surprisingly, until you really think about it, they tend to speak in what some would consider clichés:

"This isn't rocket science."

"This is a people business."

"It's all about relationships."

"We treat our employees well."

Oh please. Come on. Surely business in this day and age has gotten complicated enough to get past those old chestnuts of wisdom, hasn't it? For crying out loud, I halfway expect them to start saying, "We just play it one game at a time," or "There is no 'I' in team, Joe."

For those of you who insist that *it is rocket science* and that there's much, much more to winning in business than people and relationships, here's a flash for you. *You are wrong.* That's not me talking. That's the numbers talking. That's the market talking.

Most important of all, that's the customer talking. Believe me, I have no interest whatsoever in weaving a tapestry of warm, fuzzy stories to warm the cockles of your heart or bring a tear to your eye. I couldn't care less about that. I am a bottom line guy, and I'm interested in one thing: Does it work?

For 25 years as a consultant to and observer of some of the best companies in the world, I have reached the undeniable, righteous, whether-you-like-it-or-not conclusion that about 90 percent of what leads to success in the marketplace falls under what I call the *Five Drivers*. These are the factors that take companies to that proverbial "next level" of performance. They are the factors that differentiate and create market winners. And they are the factors that can make you indispensable and can help you become the company that your customers can't live without.

Please note carefully that I said that the Five Drivers account for about 90 percent of what works. I'm talking about those factors that go beyond the minimal, baseline requirements to be in business in the first place. Of course, you have to have a good product. You have to offer a competitive price. You have to provide good service. That's not what this book is about. Anybody and everybody offer a competitive product, price, and service, and it doesn't interest me to go there. And don't start thinking I'm saying that they're not important. They *are* important. They are the minimal, baseline requirements.

Further, if you have a superior product or one so unique that no one else offers it, you've got a monster differentiator and the world is yours. Likewise on lowest price. If you can win on price and make the numbers work, then you win big. Ditto on service. If you offer a service that nobody else is capable of offering then the world will beat a path to your door. The fact is, however, that for 99 percent of us, the competition does offer a comparable product, price, and service. So if we're going to win and get to that level of indispensability with your customers, we've got to go beyond.

No Template

At this point, I would suspect that some of you are close to rolling your eyes and saying, "Hey, don't give me the same old stuff. I want something else! I want something different!" Do you know why you want something else? Because you either can't or won't do what works. It's too hard for you. It takes too much work. It takes too much creativity. What you want is a 10, no, wait, a 20-step template (after all, more steps are better) that you can lay on your business and have endless, mindless meetings about and stew and strategize over. And you know what? You will still be stuck where you are because there isn't a 20-step template. There are the Five Drivers. Every successful company I've encountered has used them to get to the top of the heap and there's no way around it. They are the same whether you're in the consumer retail arena or are, like me, in a strictly business-to-business market. It's the same whether you're in insurance, restaurants (I own one), manufacturing, health care, consulting (what I do), airlines, manufacturers of screws (I've worked with the Screw Manufacturers Association), selling or making cars, accounting, baking, or candlestick making.

If you want to get beyond where you are stuck, then at some point you have to stop saying, "But that won't work," or "But it's not that simple," or "Give me something new," and get to work on the Five Drivers. Go do the work. Remember, this isn't my opinion. The companies in this book are successful. From Target to Oprah. Wait a minute. Did he just say Oprah? As in Oprah Winfrey? You bet I did. Think your numbers can match hers? Excuse me while I slap my belly and laugh until I cry. This woman doesn't just create big numbers. She creates great big GAUDY numbers. There are incredible lessons to be learned from Oprah, and we're taking a look at her company along with many others.

What's Your Version?

One thing that will come up over and over in this book is the need for you to have the ability to learn from someone other than another company that does what you do. If you only want to copy your more successful competitor, hey, have at it. Knock yourself out. Benchmark the most successful companies in your industry, try and copy them, and be prepared to continue to eat their dust. Let's do a reality check. You do not catch and pass your competitor by copying them. You only continue to lag behind. The best sparks for ideas that will put you in the lead in your market are probably to be found outside your market. Look at what companies completely unlike yours are doing to succeed. It's not for the purpose of copying them, either. What you have to do is look at what they're doing and continually say, "What's my version of that?" The simple process of figuring that out will lead to innovations that you never would have thought of otherwise.

So get ready to benchmark some businesses you've probably never considered. But you've got to be creative. This isn't for small minds or those who seek refuge in the whine of "Just tell me what to do." Sorry. Not that easy. If I could tell you what to do then, believe me, this book would have cost you one hell of a lot more than it did. No, what I can do is show you what works, time and time again in market after market, and then say, "There. Now you go figure out how that idea can work in your business." If you can't figure it out, you've got big problems. Business, when done well, is an extremely creative endeavor, and it's not for sissies. Business is an art form. You've got to become an artist. You've got to graduate from the paint by numbers clown face to creating your own masterpiece.

The Five Drivers

So. Enough of this pep talk. Let's get to the Five Drivers. I call them drivers because they are all ideas that drive behaviors that result in becoming indispensable. Here they are:

1. Create and sustain momentum.
2. Develop habitual dependability.
3. Continuous connection.
4. Big picture outcome.
5. Engage, enchant, and enthrall.

Rather than fill two hundred pages with an academic treatise on the theory behind each Driver, we're going to the streets. Throughout this book, we'll be looking at lots of examples and case studies of companies that have become indispensable. Their customers feel like they can't live without them. This book is about practical lessons in "How did they do that?" Virtually every lesson falls under one or more of the Five Drivers.

My clients and readers have told me over and over that they want to learn from examples of real companies. The Five Drivers give us a simple reference or touch point system. Be aware that the Five Drivers don't work in a linear fashion with one step neatly following the other. They intertwine and mix and mingle and it's a messy, organic approach to doing business. Believe me, I'd love to give you a nice neat step-by-step system but I can't find one that works. The Five Drivers "stew" works and it works every time but it's a messy process. If you really need something that you can neatly graph, plot, chart, and list, then you won't like the Five Drivers. It really is a stew. It bubbles and boils and everything takes place at the same time in a most creative and satisfying way. It's satisfying because (1) it's a fun approach to business and, even better (2) it works with customers and will make you lots of money.

This is largely a book about culture. It's a book of stories. What I attempt to do is paint a picture of what it looks like to become indispensable. Let's also note that there are a ton of other things that go into making a business successful that aren't covered in this book, like hiring, distribution, advertising, and on and on. And this is not a numbers book.

If you want to know what makes a great performer tick, you don't study the stats, you study the person. Numbers don't get to the why and the how of it all. So let's take a brief look at each of the Five Drivers, and then we'll get into the juicy stuff, which are the stories of the companies that make the Drivers work to create extraordinary customer loyalty.

Rather than organize the book with a chapter on each of the Five Drivers, I've woven them in throughout the case studies and examples. That's the way it works in the real world. All of the Five Drivers are coming into play all of the time, and you simply can't separate them out as consecutive steps. It's like one of the variety acts on the old *Ed Sullivan Show*. There was that guy who would have rings flying around one arm, spinning plates with the other, a seal balanced on his head, while his foot beat a bass drum. The Five Drivers work kind of like that. It's all happening at once.

Create and Sustain Momentum

Perhaps the biggest challenge that most companies face is organizational inertia. This is the tendency of a group of people to keep doing whatever they've been doing because it's always worked. The problem is that whatever you're doing that appears to be working may be the very thing that's keeping you from getting to the next level. To generate upward, progressive movement toward a new level of performance will usually mean letting go of what used to work in order to make room for what will work next. This is hard. This takes courage.

Markets constantly change, along with technology, customers, the economy, your competition, and just about everything else in your world. To create and sustain the momentum necessary to realize the opportunity from that change requires a couple of very simple and very difficult actions. First, you have to decide to go. Most companies don't.

If you make a decision to go to Las Vegas tomorrow, you'll go. You'll buy your plane ticket, make your hotel reservations and in the morning you'll drive to the airport, get on the plane, and go. That's called *creating momentum*. It's simply taking action that leads toward reaching the desired goal. In business, that's not the approach most companies take.

Most companies talk about going to that next level, have meetings about it, fill flip charts with ideas on how to get there, then go back to working on whatever they were doing before and life goes on as usual. It would be like you looking at brochures about Las Vegas and telling all your friends that you're going, but never buying a plane ticket. Companies do the same thing.

To create and sustain momentum means deciding to go, assigning the responsibility for the trip to someone, and then taking the action necessary to make it happen. Simple. Excruciatingly simple. And most companies can't or won't do it. It's a mystery, isn't it? I ask successful leaders how they create and sustain momentum and they say "We assign someone to make it happen, give them the authority and budget to do it, and we go."

Laggards don't like that approach. It's too simple. They would much prefer that it be terribly complicated to create momentum, because then they'd have a better excuse for not doing it. Hey, let go of your need for rocket science. Accept the simplicity of it, and get on with it.

Creating and sustaining momentum is pretty much what leadership is all about. The leaders of great companies see their jobs as keeping everyone on track and moving. It's not just what they do in the Monday morning meetings or in the occasional memo. Keeping the organization on track and moving is what they do all the time. They see it as their job. Period. And once again the mediocre performers will say that there's much more to leadership than that. Nope. Once again: Leadership is about keeping everyone on track and moving. Leadership is about sustaining momentum. You'll see how it works in the examples throughout the book.

Develop Habitual Dependability

This one is of monster importance because it gets to the heart of becoming indispensable. Consistency of performance is the great customer magnet. Inconsistency of performance is a customer repellent. Companies that command customer loyalty are nothing if not habitually dependable. Getting it right in the same way every time with a level of great service from every employee in every location without fail is the glue that holds an indispensable company together.

Here's where the Five Drivers start to intertwine. There's no way to really separate the development of habitual dependability from creating and sustaining momentum. Both of them fall under the responsibility of leadership. All of the case studies we researched made developing habitual dependability a priority. There was a constant and intense focus on reliability and steadiness. The idea is that your customer can never, ever be subject to a "depends on who you get" game of chance when doing business with you.

There's a particular cashier at a grocery store where I shop on a semi-regular basis. This guy is always personable, helpful, and professional. He has developed habitual dependability. The problem is that many of his coworkers haven't. So while this one guy might be indispensable, his company isn't. This grocery store is in a location that's very convenient for me, and their one competitor in the area doesn't seem to have a single employee that I've found is dependable in any way other than being dependably surly.

What my hope, and the hope of many in our neighborhood is, is that a Publix store may soon be built in the area. For a lot of customers, Publix has become indispensable, and a big part of their appeal is habitual dependability. While even the best of companies will have something fall through the cracks once in a blue moon, Publix has got the dependability driver pretty well nailed down.

One tip-off that a company is in trouble with this Driver is if customers find themselves going on a scavenger hunt for the good employee. I recently called our insurance company wanting information about our employee medical coverage. The first person I spoke with told me that, under our present policy guidelines, I wouldn't be able to do what I wanted to do. I hung up the phone and immediately dialed their 800 number again. I was just looking for someone different to speak with. Bingo. Another person checked my policy and told me that with a simple notation in my file, we'd be able to do what we liked.

Happy ending? Not really for me and certainly not for them. This is a company in trouble, whether they know it or not. I don't find it particularly convenient to have to call back again in a search for the "right" employee to help me. I'm not anticipating changing to a new insurance company over this, but it definitely makes them vulnerable to a competitor, and it certainly keeps them out of the indispensable category with me.

Continuous Connection

This Driver is simple, powerful, and requires vigilance. Continuous connection means that you maintain contact with your customers on an ongoing basis in such a way that strengthens your relationship. The same holds true for employees. Constant communication is the watchword for indispensable companies. Make contact early and often.

We've seen a virtual revolution in the car business around continuous connection. Car dealers used to look at the back of the store operation as a profit center, selling maintenance services and oil changes with the goal of making as much money as possible on each transaction. Now many dealers see these operations as their chief means of maintaining continuous connection with the customer with the goal of locking in loyalty and becoming indispensable.

You don't try and make money on the oil change, you give it away. Make routine maintenance services free of charge as something that comes with the purchase of the car. Get the customer back into the dealership on a regular basis, treat them like royalty, give the salesperson a chance to reconnect, and you've generated another car sale.

I'm living proof that continuous connection can work. I just spent a big chunk of money on a new car. I bought it from Thoroughbred Motorcars, the same dealer from whom I purchased my previous car. While there were any number of other car makes that I might have been happy with, I wasn't willing to give up my dealer, specifically Jeff Escue, the salesman I worked with on both cars. I wasn't willing to give up the service department either. It's been my continuous connection with the dealer through the service department and all of the free maintenance work they've done that cinched the deal for them.

Continuous connection is the Driver that indispensable companies use to keep from taking good customers for granted. You have to build in a process that constantly forces you to ask the question, "What have we done for them lately?" Neglect is a terrible mistake to make in business, and yet without a system in place to assure continuous connection, what you thought was a locked-in customer can suddenly become the topic of a "I can't believe they left us" postmortem conversation after they've taken their business to a competitor.

Big Picture Outcome

For my money, this may just be the single most powerful of the Five Drivers. While all are necessary, the ability to see the big picture outcome is the Driver that can serve as your primary differentiator from your competitor. This Driver is one of adopting a particular perspective and taking actions with the customer based on that perspective. In a nutshell, big picture outcome means the overall experience that your customer wants. It goes beyond product or service and opens up possibilities for new ways to do business.

In my own business, I've completely shifted from a transactional, event-based perspective to one of seeing the big picture outcome. I do a lot of speaking at conventions as a significant part of my business. For years, I defined my job as helping my client create a successful event. But the buying motives in that business have changed just like in virtually every other market. Buyers today have broader needs. Today, my speeches are marketed as a way to help a company become more successful. The speech is no longer the product, it's a delivery system for the product, which is ideas and strategies to make my clients more competitive. A big picture outcome is what I endeavor to create for every client I work with, even if all I do is give a speech at their convention.

Instead of looking at your product or service at the transactional level, focusing on such things as saving your client money, or ease of use, or quality, take a big picture outcome view. Think in terms of how your product or service can help your customer achieve his or her overall long-term goals. Of course, you'll have to do the work of understanding what that customer's long-term goals are, and that's work that most people aren't willing to do. But there's your competitive edge. In my business, there is no higher compliment or indicator of customer satisfaction than to have him say "You get us. More than anyone we deal with, you understand who we are, what we're about, and what we're trying to do here." Knowledge, specifically knowledge about your customer, is truly power. Do the work.

The more you look at what you do in terms of creating a big picture outcome for your customers, the more you'll develop differentiators beyond providing what customers expect from any supplier. As an insurance company, for example, you'll move up the chain of customer-influencing factors from such entry-level attributes as being financially sound, having competitive products, and giving good service, to the truly competitive factor of becoming a trusted financial advisor.

You'll see examples of seeing the big picture outcome throughout the book. Pay particular attention to these stories, because I think they get to the core issue in business today: how to differentiate. In a market where customer expectations are sky-rocketing, being able to create a compelling big picture outcome for your customer is invaluable. It is the foundation of becoming indispensable.

Engage, Enchant, and Enthrall

This Driver is the opposite of rocket science. This is magic. Only truly successful companies that understand how business really works believe in the magic of being able to engage, enchant, and enthrall customers. But, of course, that's what makes them successful. The mediocre and the struggling don't have the talent to create magic. More likely what they don't have is the creativity or the vision to pull it off. All they know is to do it by the numbers.

At number one hair-cutting chain Great Clips, this Driver is known as the *Wow factor,* and they beautifully define it as something that you do, that you don't have to do, that the customer doesn't expect you to do. This Driver works hand in hand with creating a big picture outcome, and the effect on customer satisfaction and loyalty is truly incredible.

Here's a Great Clips example. In their files are letters from satisfied customers, and one story clearly illustrates the engage, enchant, and enthrall Driver. A mom had brought her little girl in for a haircut, and the stylist was confronted with a little head of the curliest, kinkiest, and most unmanageable hair she'd ever seen. What the child clearly needed was some of the detangling spray. The mom had only enough money for the haircut, so the stylist bought a bottle of the spray with her own money and gave it to the mom to take home.

There are a lot of people who would say "That's sweet. Really precious. I'm getting all misty-eyed. But you can't stay in business by giving away your product." This is the point of view held by people whose strategy is to maximize the revenue from each transaction. What the Great Clips stylist realized was that it is far smarter to sacrifice revenue on the transaction in the interest of creating a revenue stream from a loyal and very satisfied customer, possibly for life. Great Clips would call this a Wow experience. I call it being able to engage, enchant, and enthrall your customer.

You can become indispensable and create intense loyalty to an entire brand through the engaging, enchanting, and enthralling actions of one employee. A friend of mine was on a Continental flight from Newark to Baltimore. A massive storm rolled in just as the plane pushed back from the gate and made its way onto the runway. She said that as the minutes ticked by the passengers became understandably restless. The pilot came on the public address system, informed them that it looked like they were in for a long wait, and promised to keep them updated every 20 minutes, whether he had received any new information or not.

Not only did this pilot keep his 20-minute update promise, he came out of the cockpit and assisted the flight attendants in handing out blankets and pillows. He engaged in conversations with the passengers, and generally set the tone for the entire experience. "It was amazing," my friend told me. "What would have normally been a very tense, uncomfortable situation was turned into almost a party by the actions of this pilot. The guy was absolutely great." She said that instead of being surly, the passengers began talking, sharing cell phones, showing each other baby pictures, and generally making lemonade out of this batch of lemons they'd been handed.

The ultimate duration of the runway wait was over four hours. At one point, the pilot said that he had gotten permission to return to the gate to let off any passengers who wanted to spend the night in Newark and try again in the morning. He assured them that he was going to get the plane to Baltimore that night, but that it would be very, very late. Only a handful of passengers got off the plane. The rest dug in and eventually made it to Baltimore.

My friend said that in spite of being exhausted in the middle of the night waiting for a nonexistent taxi at the Baltimore airport, she was in a really good mood. She further says to anyone who hears the story that she absolutely loves Continental Airlines and will be their customer for life. Engage, Enchant, Enthrall your customers and reap the benefits.

I see a story like this and immediately think of my own business, and whether or not I'm doing my version of that with my corporate clients. One of my favorite examples of this Driver was an information technology consulting firm I worked with that declared that "it is our professional responsibility to be absolutely delightful." The idea is to be the best part of each customer's day. This is simply the strategy of finding your edge. In an intensely competitive market, your ultimate tie-breaker is to be able to engage, enchant, and enthrall your customer. Learn it. Do it. Live it.

3

Case Study: Deluxe

Deluxe Makes Checks

"Deluxe makes checks." When you go to the Deluxe web site, those are the first words that you see. It's about as straightforward and simple a description of a company as I've ever seen. There's a very good chance that right now, in your briefcase, back pocket, or purse, you've got some checks from Deluxe that you ordered through your bank.

Here's the complete company description from the Deluxe web site: "Deluxe makes checks. Personal checks that match your passion and business checks and forms for your small business. Deluxe offers check printing, check accessories, business cards and stationery, forms and other products for small business. Deluxe checks are the most popular checks in the world."

You can say that checks are, or at least used to be, an indispensable product. But the operative words are, "used to be." While there's no question that our society is still a long, long way from becoming paperless, there's no doubt that checks are a commodity that is in decline. There's more use of credit and debit cards, direct deposit, and billing into and out of checking accounts. All of this can spell trouble for a company that is in the business of printing checks, no matter how great those checks might be.

What fascinates me about Deluxe is that it's a company that has faced its declining market reality head on and is undertaking a quite remarkable process with its customers to redefine its place in that market. The idea is that Deluxe can be much more than a check printer to the financial institutions it serves. Deluxe can become the indispensable knowledge resource for the industry. Exactly what would that look like?

That's what Deluxe is finding out on this journey with its customers. Look for the principles of all of the Five Drivers throughout this case study. The two that are particularly noteworthy here are continuous connection and big picture outcome.

I interviewed Chuck Feltz, president, Deluxe Financial Services, to find out more about the thinking behind this most unusual process, as well as to explore his thoughts on how companies can transcend commodity, overcome inertia, and redefine themselves not just by what they sell, but by who they are.

Getting beyond Commodity

Calloway: When you look at your business, which could be considered a nuts-and-bolts commodity business, how do you get it beyond that? You seem to define your business as being a lot more than the product that you sell.

Feltz: Our business is more than just the core ink-on-paper product we sell. At the core level, we must provide world-class levels of accuracy, timeliness, and consistency. This is baseline fulfillment and has to be a given in our business and has been for 90 years.

Beyond that, we try to add value by taking on more of the merchandising aspects of the program for the FI [financial institution]. Here we develop significant expertise in customer segmentation, retail pricing, and consumer buying behavior relative to our products that an FI would never try developing because their key focus is on efforts to sell more of their own products, which is where it should be. That's where they make their money. To the extent we create more return for FIs by virtue of leveraging our assets on their behalf, we can distinguish ourselves. We refer to this as "core versus context"; a concept Geoffrey Moore talks about in his book, *Living on the Fault Line* (New York: HarperCollins, 2000). Checks are a necessity for FIs to provide, but not an area they would develop deep vertical expertise in because check sales are not how they improve their value to key stakeholders. It is however, exactly how we make our living and create value for our stakeholders. So we construct our strategy to invest in our specialized areas to make the FIs more profitable and better in the eyes of their clients and then have the FIs leverage our check merchandising expertise, which is "core" for us.

Our research and work have shown us that if we add the right knowledge and value to the check program for the FI, we can also begin to affect more significant issues the FI deals with, like customer retention, satisfaction, and improving the image of their brand in the eyes of their customers, in an effort to make us more indispensable to the FI.

The Deluxe Knowledge Exchange Series

I break from the interview here to give you a description of the Deluxe Knowledge Exchange Series, which is an ongoing, complimentary series exclusive to Deluxe customers in 2004. The theme of the series is "Transforming the Customer Experience."

They've selected this theme because Deluxe's proprietary research shows that this is the number one business concern for financial institutions. Each quarter they use the Knowledge Exchange publication, web seminars, and audio conferences to focus on one of four critical steps to success in transforming the FI's customers' experiences. The Deluxe Knowledge Exchange Collaborative joins together Deluxe financial institution customers and combines their collective knowledge and experience, to explore ways to improve their customer's experience. Note that this effort exactly matches the big picture outcome Driver.

Why Would You Do That? What's in It for You?

Feltz: We chose to underwrite this program because it is a clear representation of our vision to be the model partner in the financial services industry. We believe if you put your client first and invest in ways that improve their standing with their clients, that is the essence of being the model partner. As a result, we believe our FIs, their clients, and Deluxe will benefit.

I have to admit, there was some skepticism at first. People said, "Wait a minute; you're underwriting something that has nothing to do with checks per se—why would you do that?" To us it's very clear. Put your customers' key issues at the center of your focus, invest to help them solve them, and everyone benefits. Our operating model is "on your behalf," meaning we work for the FI in a "behind the scenes" mode to support their brand with their clients. Our focus is on our clients; producing outstanding check products is one way we live out that focus. It is important we expand our focus and ability to impact key strategic fit issues if we want to grow our relevancy and value to FIs for the next 90 years of our existence.

By creating the Deluxe Knowledge Exchange and the subset called the Collaborative, our team has created an incredibly rich environment for executive interaction and relationship building that surpasses anything we have ever done. The power of working side by side with key clients on central strategic issues has been exhilarating. As one Collaborative member said, "I view Deluxe in a whole new light now and I am a committed customer for life." We could not dream of a better testimony.

We are already seeing that one of the key outputs from this will be new products and solutions. Most importantly, they are solutions constructed from the partnering of ideas and collaboration created in this new forum. It is real-time codevelopment grounded in working together on the toughest issues our clients face. And we're working on them with the executives who are accountable to address them and put solutions into place.

Calloway: So this, then, actually is driving the development of new products and services?

Feltz: Absolutely. New products, services, deeper relationships with clients and clearer insight into core strategic issues our clients wrestle with are all anticipated and expected outcomes.

Creating Relevance to the Customer

Calloway: My experience is that on paper, every bank and just about every other business is a customer's dream. Every vision and mission statement I see is just darn near perfect. So what's the disconnect between the great intentions of the vision and the reality of it just not happening? I maintain that it's a lack of process. Everybody's intentions are great, but after the big motivational meeting when you get back to business, it's nobody's responsibility to make it happen. It's a lack of process and reinforcement and even enforcement.

Feltz: I would agree that process is a key component. Process, context, communication, and reinforcement together help create the link between vision and attainment.

I would also say that leadership, as in so many cases, will ultimately decide the fate of the vision. We believe it is the obligation of our leaders to develop and constantly reinforce, through action and discussion with our associates, the link between what we do every hour of every day and how that ties to where we want to take the company. This is work that never ends. We must create this focus constantly. We feel there are two powerful ways to accomplish this. First, be in front of our associates as much as possible to create the link between our daily actions and how those roll up to a grander purpose/vision. We can't assume the link is always 100 percent obvious to everyone and so we need to create the forum and opportunities to have these very real and engaging discussions.

Second, make certain our investments support the direction. Few things send a more powerful message of vision and mission support than the manner in which we spend our capital and human resources.

When people have the opportunity to ask questions and engage the leaders in discussions about our vision and the key role that they play and then see our resources decked accordingly, we have gone a long way to fill that gap of intention versus delivery that you talked about. I'd like to say we're 100 percent there now, but that would be an overstatement because of the dynamic nature of this effort. Nonetheless, it is top of mind for us everyday.

An example of this alignment is our DeluxeSelect^{SM} program where we talk to an FI's customer directly to take their check order so the FI doesn't have to and can spend more time focusing on building their relationship with their customers who use their core services.

Doing this required a complete recalibration of our call center model to shift from a service to sales environment. This meant capital and technology improvements, complete changes in the compensation and incentive structure, and a significant change in our hiring and performance measurement. In all, a restructuring of the customer care culture.

The message was clearly, "We are taking a new direction to help our clients be better in the eyes of their customers because we believe this is the essence to becoming their model partner." To your point, significant new processes were developed, implemented, measured, and complied with and our significant investments in people and technology were a consistent message from the leadership that we were clear in striving to make our vision a reality.

Calloway: It's interesting because the approach that you're taking with the banks is to say instead of focusing on checks and how we can sell you more of those, let's focus on you, and how we can make you more successful.

Feltz: This is exactly what we hope to do. To be clearly versed in our clients' issues beyond a great check program and to align/develop our assets in a manner that creates real solutions in those areas and contributes to their overall effectiveness and value with their customers. If it's done well, there should be benefits for all stakeholders.

Calloway: In a way the whole Deluxe Knowledge Exchange and Collaborative effort is actually modeling with the banks what they need to be doing with their customers, which is to know more and find ways to serve their customers better.

Feltz: While we're not in the business of telling our clients how they should behave, we have been very fortunate to receive feedback from many of our clients that says they appreciate and respect this approach and value how it helps our relationship. We regard this feedback very highly. As one banker said, "If everyone had the goal of being our model partner, we would be unstoppable in our market." That's the kind of *WOW* statement that gets our team up every morning.

Full Accountability

Calloway: There are some people who will look at the model of what you're doing at Deluxe or they'll read a book of mine about what great companies are doing and just take the ideas and run with them. They apply their own creativity and energy to the concept and figure out how to make it work for them. They just needed somebody to flip the switch with some great ideas. There are others that say "This is no help. Where's the diagram with Step One, Step Two, and Step Three. Tell me exactly how to do it. I need a template that I can lay on top of my business and make it work." I maintain that truly great companies and truly effective leaders have the ability to figure it out. As opposed to having someone come in and do it for you or give you a step-by-step blueprint for success, as if there even were such a thing, there's something incredibly empowering about having the ownership of an idea that seems to make it work.

Feltz: It seems to us one of the first things you've got to do is to give your company permission to succeed. The environment has to support the effort, create the link to all associates, and clearly say, "This is where we're going." We took that step with DeluxeSelect. Our view was "we're going after this and need to be in the game. The end isn't clear today, but the direction is right and we will make changes as needed along the way." In this sense we communicated confidence in our leaders in that if we jumped in, we had the right minds, intentions, and passion to create an outcome that would be right and that we would be proud of.

Calloway: Okay, in creating DeluxeSelect and the Deluxe Knowledge Exchange and the Collaborative, you guys seem to be really good at what a lot of companies fail at, which is putting good ideas into action. There are countless corporate meetings where everybody comes out all inspired and motivated. But to go from there back to work, executing, and making it happen, seems to be an almost insurmountable leap for so many companies. You guys seem to do that. What's the key?

Feltz: The key for us has been to focus on two main enablers: direct leadership support and clear accountability.

Our leadership team took every opportunity to endorse the program and then free the right resources to create this direction. Why? Because we believe in it and because we created it; it was ours. When it was all said and done we own its success or failure.

Second, accountability for its development was given to a specifically designated team who had direct access to senior leadership for resources and support. As an example, our Collaborative program is owned by the Office of the Collaborative, a group of highly talented individuals who spend 100 percent of their time on the successful outcome of this work. There is no confusion over ownership or process issues regarding approval, funding, development, and execution. I'm not suggesting this is the formula for everyone, but it has worked well for us.

Calloway: Well it's really basic, but it's a mystery because, as you know, companies are famous for coming into a conference room like this, filling up a dozen flip charts with ideas and initiatives. At the end of the day everyone says, "Yahoo! Here we go!" Someone gathers up all the flip charts and then everyone waits for someone else to make something happen. Three months later in the cafeteria those same people are saying, "What ever happened to all that stuff we came up with in that meeting?" Why don't companies pull the trigger? Why can't they simply take the action?

Feltz: I won't be presumptive enough to answer that for all companies. But I can tell you for us, as we prepare to celebrate our 90th anniversary of being in business, we are very focused on the next 90 years. We have been blessed with a company that has created significant return to stakeholders over its life by virtue of its leadership position in its markets. It is no secret that over time, the paper check will face growing competition from electronic payment options. Our team believes the time to act on the future is while you are a healthy, vibrant company. Not when the end is in sight. We are driven by a passion to leave a legacy that establishes the foundation for our second 90 years. As I say this, I know that may sound a bit like motherhood and apple pie, but when this orientation is real and you live it everyday, nothing is more powerful.

We are still early into some of this new work, but believe in our hearts it is the right direction for our clients, employees, stakeholders, and our company.

The Expos: Repositioning the Company

Calloway: Tell me about your Expo events and what purpose they serve in helping you establish relevance with your customers.

Feltz: The Expos accomplished three objectives for us:

1. Launched our new DeluxeSelect program and gave us the forum to show that our original hypothesis about the benefits of our interacting with our FI's customers "on their behalf" was true when taken to scale; specifically that based on our extensive knowledge, and the leverage of our culture on the FIs behalf, we could actually drive the FI revenues up, their costs down, while at the same time increasing their customer's satisfaction.

2. Created a forum to deepen Deluxe and FI senior executive relationships.
3. Repositioned our brand in the context of our new vision to be the model partner in the financial services industry.

With this in mind, we gathered 400 of our top clients and prospective clients in two venues. The program consisted of an address by our chairman, and presentations by world-class experts in the area of market research, strategy, and customer satisfaction, to bring thoughts and knowledge to our clients that they could use immediately in their businesses, and finally to rollout our DeluxeSelect program including an invitation to participate, at our expense, in the Deluxe Knowledge Exchange and Deluxe Collaborative.

Calloway: Here's something interesting about culture. The nature of my work is such that I go to corporate meetings and customer events all of the time. The difference between your Expos and most corporate customer events is that a lot of your customers, when watching the rollout of the Deluxe Knowledge Exchange and the Collaborative, and all of these programs designed purely to help the banks be more successful, were waiting for the Deluxe product pitch. They were waiting for the commercial and the pitch where you ask them to buy more of your stuff. Instead of that, you had research for them and speakers like DeWitt Jones talking about being more creative in business. A lot of your customers were saying, "This is great. But what's the catch?"

Feltz: I have to admit, we did get a bit of that feedback. And it would be wrong to say we expect no return for our work. We do. In the form of stronger relationships, new services and solutions that increase our relevance over time to our clients and therefore a foundation for growth in our next 90 years of business. It's that we made the move to clearly step out and invest on behalf of our clients today, knowing we will both benefit in years to come by our taking this initial step.

Calloway: So your thinking behind the Expo programs was pretty much a capsule version of the thinking behind everything you've been talking about, which is knowing customers better and creating a culture dedicated to serving them.

Feltz: That's right. And that we would take the initiative to begin to redefine our relationship with them in this new context.

Calloway: It's almost like instead of selling something different, you *become* something different.

Feltz: That is what we're doing. It's still in development, but that's exactly what we're trying to do.

Calloway: You're having fun doing all this, aren't you?

Feltz: I think I can say that even with all the associated challenges in our market, our team has never been more stimulated and challenged, intellectually and personally. It's not often that you have a chance to participate in the repositioning of a 90-year-old company and to engage in these kinds of conversations. We're having a ball with what we're doing. This is cool, fun stuff, and though the final page is yet to be written, we're okay with that. Why? Because the client and employee feedback tells us this is the right thing for us to do. Our clients are saying "More. Keep going here. We want you to explore this with us." How can you not love that?

As an example, we have been working with a very good client of ours on some new approaches to customer experience creation based on our success with our DeluxeSelect program. In a recent conversation, the vice chairman, who is integrally involved in this said, "We're thinking about trying some new things outside of the check program and we'd like to have Deluxe involved." I said "Well, how do you see us participating?" "I'm not sure yet," he said. "But I know I want you on this team." That's one of the greatest compliments we've ever had because they view us as participating in new solutions beyond their check program.

Calloway: Will the next version of the Expos be more of a "how to" program? More of a "Now that we're into these ideas, lets talk about implementation and execution?"

Feltz: I see three potential outcomes in the next Expo. First, a potential launch of new services and solutions that may evolve from our Collaborative work. Second, we see it as an opportunity to highlight our new strength in the small business relationships for banks, by virtue of our recent New England Business Service, Inc. acquisition. Third, and this is the key area of focus for a majority of our clients, the clients engaged in the Collaborate will report the results of the 12 months of work they are completing.

Know What the Customer Really, Really Wants

Calloway: Do you have the sense that small businesses are not happy with their bank relationships?

Feltz: Like anything else, some are and some aren't. Some FIs excel here; others feel they have room to improve. Our goal is to add value in their relationship with them no matter what their current situation. With our new breadth of knowledge and resources as a result of our NEBS acquisition, we have unparalleled strength in our industry to help our FI clients better diagnose, understand, and serve this important segment.

Calloway: Do you think that in business in general, and that buyers of almost everything, are moving toward that expectation? There will always be a place for the business that says, "We've got a thousand widgets at the lowest price, so just pick out what you want." But is there more of a movement that says, "It's not enough for you to have a product. You've got to help me choose the product and learn how to use the product."

Feltz: I think companies can make a great living in both of those spaces, but you must know where you are adding value and where you have the ability to excel. If you're doing the thousand widget thing at the lowest price, you need to know that's your business and your value proposition and which of your customers have that expectation. In some cases, applying new customer knowledge to your widget competency can lead you to new and more valuable services for your clients by providing direction to improve which products they use and how they use them. The magic comes from knowing the clients well enough to articulate the best offer to the right client. A simple notion that is powerful when properly executed.

Calloway: I've listened in on calls at your Phoenix call center, and I was amazed at how excited some check customers get when they find out about a particular feature that's available to have printed on the check. When you hit the right feature for them they say "I've GOT to have that!" Price never even comes up. And the customer is absolutely thrilled to get the feature. What do you call that kind of customer? Check enthusiasts?

Feltz: Yes, check enthusiasts. And as you know it's not everyone we talk to. But we know how many and which of our FI's customers fall into this category and that if we are focused on serving them properly, overall profits and satisfaction increase dramatically. And this is the skill and knowledge we invest in on our clients behalf, to make them better in the eyes of *their* customer.

It's the nucleus of being the model partner, and it's the essence of core versus context. And it applies beyond just our business at Deluxe.

I learned the core versus context lesson in my personal life right after I moved to Minnesota. One of the first things you have to do when you move to Minnesota is figure out how to remove up to 100 inches of snow a year from your driveway.

My first year there I figured how hard can that be? So after the first 15-inch snowfall out comes the snow blower and off I go. One night, it's 10 P.M. and I'm outside dressed in six layers of clothes clearing my driveway. One thought crept into my mind—if I freeze to death out here, do I want to be remembered as the guy with the clean driveway? No, I want to be the guy remembered for being inside with his two girls and their mom, reading stories and saying their bedtime prayers. Being a great dad is my goal for core competency, not snow blowing. A week later, more snow. By now I have sold the snow blower and found a guy who eats, sleeps, and breathes snow removal! It's his core, but it's my context so the job is his. He makes the investment, develops the knowledge and adds significant value to his life by doing this and I'm thrilled to have the time to spend developing my core. And, he and I are measurably better as a result.

Getting Employee Buy-In

Calloway: From a leadership standpoint, how do you get all of these employees spread out all over the place to keep having buy-in to what you're trying to do?

Feltz: We think it boils down to context and our leaders' ability to connect daily activities and behavior to our mission and vision. An example of that (and a normal conversation our team has all the time) took place in one of our production facilities with a woman who works in our bindery area. She physically takes the printed checks, puts them in a box, double checks the appearance of the package, and it goes out the door. Her name is Juanita. I asked her how things were going and she said, "Everything's great. You know, I'm just doing my job, putting the checks in the box and getting them to the customers."

I said, "You know Juanita, I want to give you a little different perspective on how I see what you do. You know we talk a lot about the customer experience and helping our FI customers look good to their customers." She said, "Yeah, I know, and I know that the call center people make sure that happens." I said, "Let me share with you a different view. When somebody opens that check box, what do they want to see?" She said, "They want to know that all of their checks are there and that there are no ink smudges and that it's all clean and they have the right checks."

I said, "Right, and what if that doesn't happen? Or what if we commit the cardinal sin in the check business and put someone's name on somebody else's account line on the checks?" She said, "Well that would be terrible." "And who controls a lot of that?" I asked her. She answered, "Well I try to make sure that doesn't happen."

"Right." I said, "And here's the thing. Seventy-five million times a year somebody opens one of our packages. Every time they open it the first thing they notice is what you did. That's where the customer experience starts. Not only is it an experience with us, the customer looks at this as an experience that their bank has given them. You are the last step between us and that experience."

She said she had never thought of her job in that way and seemed to stand even taller at her work area after that. The point is our team is always looking for that opportunity to re-contextualize daily behavior in the context of our vision and mission. It's the idea that all companies have a vision, but if the person who does something every day, a thousand times a day can see for themselves that every one of those thousand actions is a part of that larger, nobler purpose, all of a sudden it matters more. And I have found few people who really don't want to add value and "matter" more. That is our leaders' daily challenge, to show everyone how what they do every day matters at this high level. Helping to make that connection changes everything.

Calloway: I think that it's what's missing in a lot of companies. They talk to their people and say, "Here's your job." But they never say, "And here's the *point* of your job."

Feltz: You could take the approach and say it's Juanita's job to figure it out. We believe that it's *our* job as leaders to create a context for her and then *her* job to execute to her best ability in that context. We can't expect to take a little PowerPoint presentation out to 4,000 people and say, "Here's the vision. Okay. You got it?" It doesn't work that way. So it's our *obligation* to help Juanita see the link between what she does eight hours a day, a thousand times a day and see how we're trying to change the future of our company through her and all of her contributions. Do that for our 4,000 people and you have created a powerful force to be reckoned with in your market.

Calloway: It's all the same stuff, isn't it? What you want to do with the banks is what the banks should be doing with their customers, and what you want to do with your employees.

Feltz: Again, our clients choose their own direction. Our goal is to set a model of client dedication that is second to none.

Breaking the Inertia

Calloway: It seems like this really isn't all that hard.

Feltz: It's hard in the context of breaking the inertia of organizational thinking. That's what we constantly focus on. We are anxiously awaiting the results, because we believe it is our future.

Calloway: Is it accurate to say that even at this point in the process, you're beginning to see some positive results in customer retention?

Feltz: Yes. Absolutely. We have much more ground to cover, but participation by our clients in the Deluxe Knowledge Exchange is creating retention results that clearly justify the cost. That participation consists of signing up, getting the quarterly publication, participating in the webinars, and events like the 1-800 calls. And the bonus is that our associates are having a ball with this and know that not everyone gets the opportunity to be a part of ensuring a 90 year old company clears the way for its next 90 years.

Calloway: When you're dealing with a commodity, what choices do you have in terms of staying competitive?

Feltz: You can reprice it, you can repromote it, find a new distributor, repackage it like the people who sell yogurt have now come out with yogurt sticks. But when your product is moving toward a commodity and is slowly declining, it presents a unique challenge. Our urgency and passion around this is very high. You're catching us early in this process, and while we believe we're on the right path to discover new solutions and value for our clients, the end story is not yet complete. When people ask if that makes me uncomfortable, I say we're in this game to figure that out. And what could be better than having our clients say to us, "We want you in the game with us."

Courageous Decisions

I found the interview with Chuck Feltz to be fascinating and incredibly relevant to the concept of becoming indispensable on a number of levels. Peter Drucker has talked about successful companies making "courageous decisions." For many companies, possibly even most of them, there will come a time when, if they are to achieve or maintain indispensable status in the market, they will have to make courageous decisions. This could involve what, for many, is the most confrontive and difficult decision of all, being willing to let go of what used to work in order to make room for what will work next. This process may very well include a significant period of uncertainty. At Deluxe, they aren't sure what the next phase of their business will be. But Deluxe is willing to take the gutsy and completely necessary step of embarking on the journey to find out.

The lesson is obvious, if difficult. Make your own courageous decision. Partner with your customers to discover how you can be indispensable in tomorrow's market. Think about defining your company not by the products or services you sell, but by the successful outcomes you can create for your customers.

But Is It Working?

It's all well and good to hear the perspective of Deluxe and learn what they're trying to accomplish. The question is, "Is it working?" I believe that the market decides. At the end of the day it doesn't matter what anyone thinks except the customer.

Karen R. Makowski, senior vice president for Performance Enhancement with SouthTrust Bank, is a Deluxe customer and member of the Collaborative. I asked Karen to discuss how she feels about Deluxe's efforts to become more than just a "check vendor" to customers, and also her participation as a member of the Collaborative. Here's what Karen had to say:

> I met Deluxe when their response to SouthTrust's check vendor RFP arrived on my desk one week after I arrived at SouthTrust. Throughout the RFP decision process, Deluxe positioned themselves as more than a check vendor. We kept saying, "Hey, it's just checks, isn't it?" They proved it was more than checks.
>
> Deluxe was relentless in positioning themselves as a check vendor, a profit enhancer, a source of creative selling

ideas, and a company with a solution to checks *and* all of the issues that arise when one company sublets its precious customers to another company to service. We were blown away by their accountability: not just their senior management but line managers who said, "This is my job. I deliver great checks or great phone service or great conversion experiences for your staff."

We visited both the Deluxe manufacturing and call center operations. We witnessed a passion for the customer within every employee we talked with. Pride, ownership, and passion in every employee? How did they do this? Was it just on visitors' day? We tested it by checking their references deeply. Every reference was positive. We talked to employees in sessions and in the restrooms. They were consistently positive about the company.

Our four criteria for choosing a check vendor were:

1. Enhance the customer experience in ordering checks. Customers must be treated at least as well as we wanted and expected them to be in our own financial centers.
2. Remove nonproducing workload from our branch sales staff.
3. Improve the profitability of the bank's check program.
4. Partner with a learning organization where we can learn from them even as they service our relationship.

Deluxe hit the mark on all four and was awarded our business in February 2003 with a June 30, 2003, bankwide conversion. By the way, while the financial numbers from Deluxe were good, we passed on a more lucrative counteroffer from another bidder. In the end, it was not only about the financial impact to SouthTrust.

So, Deluxe showed us that they wanted to be more than just a check vendor from the very start. When they unveiled the Deluxe Knowledge Exchange and the Deluxe Collaborative, we were very intrigued. The Knowledge Exchange allows us to connect our financial center selling staff and general bank administration staff to world-class authors and speakers who are designing the new ways to embrace customers to create a competitive edge. It was great and it was free.

The Collaborative looked like serious learning. What a time commitment and an expense commitment for the bank! But, the topic was fascinating to us as students of customer service leadership. Could Deluxe really facilitate industry learning? How could that happen with financial institutions of so many stripes? Would this be another vendor boondoggle or would we truly learn? Lucky for me, SouthTrust was willing to give it a try and I was accepted after interviewing for the Collaborative. The interviewing alone said this was not a vendor boondoggle.

The Collaborative has been two things: very enlightening and a lot of work! Deluxe has modeled the learning as hosts of the Collaborative. They have provided an environment of learning and facilitated an honest exchange of ideas and information. The group of 12 lucky financial institutions has jelled into quite the team.

For Deluxe, the learning has been about the deep needs of their customers. And they have learned a lot about what we do well, how we operate, and what we do not do well as an industry. That has to be valuable in the retention and sale to clients. By sharing the experience of the Collaborative through their client newsletter, they are building a large following. The Knowledge Exchange web and audio sessions offered to all clients have followed some of the Collaborative themes while adding value to the Deluxe relationship at participating financial institutions. When

Deluxe unveils the results of the Collaborative pilots at their Expo, they will build broad customer validation for their effort to be more than a check vendor. I hope they will tell their story in all the trade press as well.

I also asked Karen if she felt that, in general, more companies are going to need to rethink the value that they bring to their customers? Are we all going to need to redefine the business that we're in? Are banks doing that? Karen's response:

> The economy has shifted to an experience economy and financial institutions need to wake up and smell the coffee brewing. We have to bring the customer back into focus. We have to bank on building customer value. As an industry, we have embraced segmentation, cross-sell, packaged products, technology, and CRM but we still cross our fingers every night that we have made it hard enough for customers to leave so we can retain their relationship. Who can compete on "tangle you up so it is too painful to leave" for long? This is not a growth strategy.
>
> For real growth, financial institutions and all industries have to define their purpose as one that does something valuable for customers. This will lead to engaged and loyal customers and this is how profits will be generated in a commoditized industry.
>
> This is not just banking. All businesses have to "get it" about the customer. If we focused on the customer as much as we focus on the stock analysts, imagine the potential for economic impact!
>
> Yes, I do think companies need to re-examine what they bring to the marketplace. What is the higher reason for financial institutions? I think it is to solve the financial worries of consumers and businesses. To do this in a way

that is meaningful to clients and creates passionate, purposeful, and fulfilled employees means getting down to the customers' emotional engagement with their financial institution and connecting at the "deep need bone" proving you bring more value than just a free checking account to the relationship.

4

Back to the Six New Basics

Radical Today—Basic Tomorrow

What is considered a radically innovative idea today will be to-morrow's baseline expectation. I happen to think that there really aren't very many truly radical ideas or innovations out there. What we might call outside-the-box thinking in one industry is what's been done for years in another. There's nothing wrong with that. I'm a wholehearted believer in the cross-pollenization of ideas across industry lines. I also think that most of what is considered wildly innovative thinking is usually just a new interpretation of concepts that have been around for ages.

There will be those who read this book or almost any other business book and feel frustrated that there's nothing they consider brand new in it. I feel your pain. What interests me is how real-world businesses capture market share and create loyalty with their customers. We don't get hurt by what we don't know. We get hurt by what we know but don't do. It may not be new, but it may need to be newly applied by you in your particular business.

So let's take a look at some very basic ideas. The twist here is that, for many, the ideas may be presented in a way they haven't thought of before. If it makes you think, "I've never looked at it that way before. Hmmmm. . . . Maybe in our company we could . . . ," and it leads you to a new and more effective way of doing things, then we've accomplished a great deal. That's the whole purpose of this book—to take a new look at what we do, knock the cobwebs out of our thinking, and approach our businesses with fresh ideas.

New Basic 1: Say "Why Not?" Continuously

"Some people see things as they are and say, Why? I dream things that never were and say, Why not?" I wish I'd said that, but George Bernard Shaw did. For my money it's one of the greatest business strategies ever known. Say "Why not?" Say it early. Say it often.

It's a very simple yet very confrontive notion to look at the accepted way of doing business and consider letting it go. Unlock the handcuffs that have shackled your own creativity by challenging what may seem like a "basic" in your particular business. Albert Szent-Gyorgyi, 1937 Nobel Laureate in Medicine, put it this way when he said, "Discovery consists of seeing what everybody has seen and thinking what nobody has thought."

Here's how it works. I was on the advisory board for a travel agency that was opening an office that would be devoted to the big-ticket leisure traveler. They wanted this office to be inviting and to encourage clients to spend time there and really explore the possibilities of what was available in high-end leisure travel. In one meeting while we were discussing the actual layout of the office, the agency owner said, "The counter will be here, right where people first enter the office." "Why do we need a counter?" I asked. "Because that's where people pick up their tickets or check in with the receptionist for their appointment," she replied. "But if we're trying to make this an inviting and relaxing environment, conducive to people hanging out and thinking about spending big chunks of money on a vacation, why would we greet them with a physical barrier as soon as they walk in the door?" I asked. "Well, it's just that travel agency offices usually have a counter," she said. I replied, "But why not use that space for a couch and table and chairs with high-end travel magazines and books and things that will invite them to want to have a cup of coffee and dream big expensive vacation dreams?" Which is exactly what we ended up doing. It was very successful.

A friend of mine is a regular at a restaurant in which there are no tables, booths, or counters. You sit on a couch. A big, comfy couch. The couches have tray tabletops built in that you swing out to put your plate on. It's like eating in front of the television at home, and it's captured a big following in his town. Why not couches in a restaurant? Because nobody's ever done it? That's precisely the objection that most people raise about the next innovation. We can't do it because nobody else has ever done it!

Asking "Why not?" even extends to your philosophy of management. My young friend Jason went to work as a waiter at a local restaurant. After he had been working there for a few weeks, I asked Jason, a veteran of waiting tables for a few years, how the job was going. "It's not like any restaurant I've ever worked in," he said. "My first day on the job, my manager sat me down and said that before he told me what my job duties would be, he wanted me to be clear on what *his* job duties were. He said that first and foremost his job was to make sure that my job was the best job I'd ever had." I asked Jason if the manager had really followed through on that promise. "Yes," he said. "It's like an upside-down approach compared to the other restaurants. It's like the managers work for the wait staff." Well, why not? It makes perfect sense. It's just not the way people traditionally approach managing.

If you are a rock band, instead of prohibiting tape recorders at concerts, why not invite people to tape your music to their heart's content? Build demand. Have those fans play their bootleg concert tape for their friends, who will then buy your albums and tickets for your next concert. That's what some of the biggest-grossing touring bands in history did.

If you are an extremely successful copier and printer supplier looking to sell to the top executives in growing companies, why not launch a campaign of having your sales teams call on your OWN executives and find solutions for your OWN organization's document needs? RJYoung Company did it, and it turned around their whole approach to the marketplace.

If you're a bank, why charge customers for checking accounts and ATM usage? If you're a car dealer, why charge customers for oil changes? If you're a consultant, why not give your clients unlimited access to you rather than put time limits on it? "But, but, but, but . . ." I can hear the chorus of "buts." "But that's how we make money." Well, why not use those products and services for which you've always charged to invite customers into a much more profitable relationship based on higher margin sales? "But customers will take unreasonable advantage of me." No, they won't. Every company I've ever researched that offers what seems to be an outrageous level of service, like Tractor Supply Company's guarantee that every employee is empowered to do whatever it takes to make the customer happy, has said that the number of customers who take unfair advantage is so small it hardly shows up on the radar. What does show up on the radar are the customers who make you indispensable because you are giving them service that locks them in.

The "Why nots?" are endless. Look at what you do and how you do it. Then challenge the assumption. You may go right back to what you've been doing, but at least you will have had the valuable experience of thinking it through and, at a minimum, finding ways to improve it. Why not? Why on earth would you not?

New Basic 2: Get Back Inside the Box

As a counterbalance to the new basic of saying, "Why Not?" continuously, may I suggest that before you begin to embrace all of that ever-so-popular outside-the-box thinking, you'd better be darned sure that you've taken care of everything *inside* the box. There are far too many companies saying, "Let's be different," that should be saying, "Let's be really good at what we do first, *then* we can be different!" The concept here is simple. All of the differentiation in the world will be wasted unless you have mastered your core business.

I co-own a restaurant. Job number one at that restaurant is great food. We've got that covered because of the incredible talent and expertise of Michael DeGregory, our chef and co-owner. The guy cooks like nobody's business. Our food rocks. It's our greatest strength. Next comes the front of the house and all that happens there. Colleen DeGregory, co-owner and general manager, makes it all happen the way it should in terms of service and ambiance. Most reviews refer to our restaurant as "hip." It's a very cool place.

We do a lot of things outside the box at our restaurant, but if Michael wasn't taking care of everything inside the box—the quality of the food—we'd be in trouble. It's like so many of the dot-com companies in the late 1990s. They were cool and fun and innovative and wildly creative. The only problem with so many of them was that they didn't do anything particularly well except be cool and fun and innovative and wildly creative. They spent so much time outside the box that nothing ever happened inside the box.

This applies on a personal level as well. For five years, I did a lot of work for a telecommunications company. At lunch at one of their regional sales meetings the vice president of sales was seated next to a very peppy young sales representative who proceeded to make quite a positive impression on the executive. I was also seated at that table and I was also impressed with the sales representative. This guy was blasting out ideas and strategies that caused the executive to actually take out a pad and take occasional notes.

After lunch, the executive spoke to the sales representative's manager and said how impressed he had been by the young man. He said, "This guy's got it all. He's really on the ball." His manager replied, "Yeah, he's impressive. He's got it all except for one thing. He can't sell his way out of a paper bag. He's dead last in sales for the entire region." In Texas they call that "all hat and no cattle."

The guy needs to either get in the box and learn to do some business or find himself another line of work where making a good impression can be his core activity. Maybe he's got a future in public relations or corporate communications. Whatever he does, he'd better have the core competencies covered or he's busted.

New Basic 3: You Will Partner

UPS and Mailboxes ETC partnering to become the UPS Stores. Kinko's and Federal Express. Grocery stores and banks. Target and walk-in health clinics. Who's your partner? Who's got the customers that should also be *your* customers? It may not take the form of a merger or formally structured partnership, but you will partner at some point with somebody. More likely you will partner with lots of somebodies.

The days of "Here's what I've got, and this is all I can do for you" are rapidly being replaced with "I can put together the pieces of the puzzle that will take care of you on a big picture outcome basis." This doesn't mean spreading yourself too thin or diluting your brand. It means strengthening your brand by becoming the "go-to resource" that your customers come to rely on for helping make their life better.

In the 24 years that I've been in business, what I count as one of my greatest and most profitable accomplishments is that my clients come to me for advice on things that are outside the range of services I can deliver. They trust me, and they trust my judgment. What this does is give me the opportunity to partner with other professionals whom I trust implicitly to do an extraordinary job for my clients, in order to expand my sphere of influence and increase my value to the customer.

Sometimes a company has to say, "What are we doing that we should NOT be doing?" Too often companies think that doing more is, by definition, better. Not so. Doing more can be the fatal mistake that takes a company down. Partnering with others who offer a product or service of value to your customers can make perfect sense and work for the ultimate benefit of all involved.

What other businesses in your market are complementary to yours? Give your product or service away through them. Generate interest for them and new customers for yourself. When a new barbershop opens in the neighborhood, take the doughnuts you make to them to give to every new customer they get. What's your version of this?

The traditional hunting ground for new customers is to look at your competition and say, "How can I get those customers to come to me?" Take another perspective of the hunting ground. Stop obsessing about your competition and, instead, think in terms of, "Who else do our customers do business with?" As an author, I don't think about how to take sales away from other authors. I think about what else the readers of business books buy.

Lots of banking, insurance, and other financial services professionals buy my books. So what else do they buy? How do they want to improve their position with their customers? How do my needs intersect with their needs in a way that benefits all, including the customers? When I give a bank copies of my book to give to their customers, it's then just a matter of standing back and watching the synergy take place.

The bank's customers are happy with the bank for giving them the book. Good for the bank. The bank's customers then read and, hopefully, like the book. They then order copies for their employees. Good for the customer, good for the employees, good for the bank, and good for Joe. And, like the Energizer Bunny, the ripple effect goes on, and on, and on.

A company hires me to give a presentation at its annual conference. They have invited some of their best customers to join them at the conference. Well, Joe, let's put our thinking cap on. How about if, in addition to doing the presentation for which they've contracted, I throw in joining them with their customers at the private luncheon that I see on the agenda? I'll answer some questions, give them some ideas about business, and make everybody happy. It's a total win-win-win deal. And it puts me in partnership with my client in a way that puts me in the path of their clients and the ripples begin again.

Remember that this isn't about getting into businesses where you don't belong. It's about partnering, perhaps in a virtual way or on an event basis, with a company that can expose you to market circles that you've previously left untapped. Start with this question: Who else do my customers do business with? Go from there.

New Basic 4: Selling Is Dead

Traditional selling skills will continue to die a slow and much deserved death. Such techniques as overcoming objections and developing a "power close" will become even more obsolete than they already are. I think that sales guru Jeffrey Gitomer, whom I use as a case study elsewhere in this book, would agree with me.

The idea that selling is talking someone into buying your product is a concept that has largely disappeared and will be totally dead very soon. Good riddance. It's a cumbersome and inefficient way to create customers.

Here's where we're going, and I would think that most of you are already there. If you are, go further down this road. If you're not, wake up and smell reality. I don't sell anything to anybody. Ever. If someone asks me, "Why should I do business with you?" I have the same answer for everyone. I say, "I don't know that you should. That's what we have to find out." Again, for some of you this is a basic that you embraced long ago. But for many, it's sacrilege. It seems an outrageous, naïve, and gimmicky statement.

No. It's simply a recognition that the way people make buying decisions has changed. If your prospects are businesses, and you know everything about what you do and not much about what they do, then you're toast, my friend. The old days of getting the appointment to make your presentation and then waiting to overcome objections are so yesterday's news that it hurts. You should know so much about the prospect's business going in that if you get to the point where you make an appointment, the subsequent agreement to do business is already practically a done deal.

The whole idea that selling is a numbers business still holds true, but it's a different set of numbers today. You go spend your time making sales calls. Go make 50 in one week. Then be happy with your three closed sales. I'll spend my time preparing and learning infinitely more than you about the prospect's business. I'll have seven conversations. And I'll close six sales.

This reassessment in what makes for effective selling is simply part of understanding and using the Driver called big picture outcome. You match the right copier with the customer according to how that copier can help accomplish the customer's business objectives. You match the right soft drink according to how it can help the customers accomplish the lifestyle and health goals that they've set. Give me the diet, no caffeine, cherry, low-carb cola. In the short can. Twelve-pack refrigerator stack, please.

Selling is dead. Matching is alive and well and thriving. As Jeffrey Gitomer says, "It's not about selling. It's about people buying." That's a whole new ballgame. If you can change your language to reflect more of a value placement approach to business, you'll beat the pants off of your competitor who's out there selling. Let me stress that this is not semantics. This is a new perspective. Reality is how you look at it. Embrace the new reality of how people buy, and you can become indispensable.

New Basic 5: Whatever Happens Is Normal

We've all been so bombarded by the whole subject of change in the past 10 years that I think you're probably like me. You're sick of it. There are certain business magazines that seem to run the same cover stories every month:

"Living In a World of Change!"

"Change! Get Used to It!"

"The Opportunity of Change!"

"Change or Die!"

Okay, enough already. We've got it. Everything changes all the time and we have to adapt to it in order to succeed. Fine.

The old basic is being able to change and adapt during hard times. The new basic is that there are no hard times. There are just times. If you stop putting a value judgment on whether what's happening is good or bad, then you're much more able to use it. I'm not talking about war, hurricanes, or death and destruction hard times. Those truly are hard times. I'm talking about a challenging economy, high interest rates, new government regulations, competitive threats, technological revolutions, and the like. Nothing hard about those times. They just are what they are. Here's the mantra that works: *Whatever happens is normal.*

Think about two people that you work with. Pick one who is the office whiner. Nothing suits him. Nothing goes his way. The slightest change in the market throws him totally off. If the competition lowers price, then he cries, "Ye gods! This isn't normal! It's apocalypse now!" If interest rates go up and tighten buying activity, it's, "This isn't normal! It's Armageddon!" To him, the only times that are "normal" are times that are easy. Think about his worth to the company and his effectiveness in the marketplace. It's pretty much nil on both counts. Loser.

Contrast that person with the one who is cool, effective, and will handle whatever the market throws at her. Price war going on? She says, "Well, let's not play that game, and here's what we'll do to whip the price cutters." Economy tightening? She says, "Fine. The market's been too hot, and too many competitors have gotten into this game that have no business here. A tight market will thin the herd. Here's what we'll do."

I see this contrast between people all the time when I travel. Take cancelled flights, for example. I see them as normal. I don't like them. I wish they didn't happen. But anybody who travels even a moderate amount will tell you that cancelled flights are normal. Delayed flights are even more normal. By seeing it that way, I have the advantage of not going ballistic. I simply do the normal things one does in order to find an alternate way to get to my destination. In the meantime, there will be those who go completely nuts when the cancellation or delay is announced. To them, this isn't normal; therefore they shouldn't be expected to handle it. Instead of simply solving the problem, they feel justified in launching into a mindless tirade about the inefficiencies of the evil airlines. While they throw their tantrums, I make other arrangements.

This isn't rah-rah, motivational, positive thinking stuff. It's about being pragmatic and nonemotional about the reality of how things work. It's about being able to live in the world as it is and figure out how to make yourself indispensable to the customer regardless of what's going on. I can't imagine a more straightforward and reasonable way of looking at the world. Save the angst and heartache for something that really deserves it, like hunger and war and natural disasters. But why get torqued out over business as usual?

All of this is pure perception. Make no mistake about it, your perception IS your reality. There is no way for you to look at the world except through your own particular perception. Indispensable performers see the world in a way that creates confidence. My favorite NFL team, since I live in Nashville, is the Tennessee Titans. Steve McNair, the Titans quarterback, was voted along with Peyton Manning of the Indianapolis Colts, Co-Most Valuable Player in the NFL for the 2003/2004 season. What makes them so valuable, even indispensable, to their teams? One reason is that there is no panic in them. They can be down by 21 points in the fourth quarter with three minutes left to play, and they still expect to win. It's not a false "whistling through the graveyard" optimism. It's an optimism based on knowing what to do and then executing it.

The key is that, just like in business, McNair and Manning see that do-or-die scenario in the closing minutes of a game as being normal. They don't particularly like it. They'd much rather have a comfortable lead. But it's NORMAL. Therefore, they perform.

Watch the flight attendants on your next really bumpy flight. The plane can be bouncing like a ping-pong ball, and they'll be calm as can be, reading or talking with their coworkers, as are the frequent flyers, while the occasional flyers are bordering on panic. Bumpy flights are normal. If the flight attendants start to scream, then I'll join in. Before that point, it's all normal.

I find indispensable the business professionals who, when confronted with a challenging assignment, convey calm and absolute mastery of the situation. If you are a vendor working for me and say things like, "Oh, man. I don't know how we're going to make this work. This is really tough!" then you're not likely to be working for me for very long. If, on the other hand, I present you with a challenge and you say, "Fine. Let's see how we're going to make this happen for you." That's indispensable. Don't panic on me. Do your job. If it was easy, I'd do it myself and wouldn't need you in the first place.

A final word on what's normal. Not having all the information is normal. You'll never have all the information. Not knowing what's going to happen next is normal. When you do forecasting, you must do it with the clear understanding that whatever you come up with, you're going to be wrong. If you know that in advance, then you can proceed accordingly and gain some valuable knowledge but not get bent out of shape when the world changes unexpectedly. When you face making an important decision, you must make it with the clear understanding that you will never have all the information necessary to make the perfect decision. The bottom line is that you may think you understand the situation, but the situation just changed. It's not so much about making perfect decisions as making the best decision you can, and then moving on to the next best decision very quickly. In other words, you set your course, and then you change direction. That's normal.

New Basic 6: The Internet Didn't Change Anything

This is one that will get some folks riled up. The foaming-at-the-mouth Internet evangelists who tend to speak about the power of the Internet in a never-ending string of superlatives all followed by exclamation marks will find this New Basic to be very upsetting. Sorry. The Internet didn't change anything. At least not anything that truly matters.

If you had been frozen in 1955 and thawed out in 2005, you would doubtless have been amazed at all the wondrous things that have taken place. We've been to the moon; gas pumps accept credit cards; everyone's got a computer and a cell phone and a Blackberry; fax machines can send messages anywhere; ATMs give you money wherever you are; and you can do business on the Internet. Wow. All cool. And it's obviously just a tiny sampling of the incredible technological achievements in the past 50 years.

But the fax machine was supposed to make companies like FedEx and UPS obsolete. Didn't happen. Computers were supposed to result in the paperless office. Ha. Double ha! Video-conferencing was supposed to eliminate the need for meetings where people all sat in the same room together. Nope. All of these things have changed the *way* we do business, but they haven't changed the basic nature or rules of doing business.

The Internet was supposed to replace all other forms of advertising. Remember when all the talk was about how many "eyeballs" a web site attracted? Gazillions of dollars were spent on banner ads to those eyeballs with the end result being that the eyeballs didn't buy anything. Oops, there's that pesky rule of business again: At some point somebody's got to buy something, or you'll go out of business. The Internet didn't change that.

What other basic rules of business haven't changed in the Internet age? Pretty much all of them, including the need to make your customer's experience a good one, whether it's in your store, on the phone, or on your web site. It still has to be easy to do business with you. You still have to discover your customer's needs. You still have to offer a quality product or service at a competitive price.

For all the talk a few years ago by the wild-eyed zealots who declared the rest of the world to be hopeless luddites if they didn't embrace the Internet and the "new economy" and tear down their existing business model, business is still business. We still make things and sell them. Everything I'm saying here is in the interest of gaining perspective. My point here is that you should never make your web site the point. The web site is a means to an end, which is serving the customer.

I spoke in New Orleans to a convention of newspaper web site designers and managers. I was about the only nontechnical speaker on the agenda, and I think the audience wasn't quite sure what I had to say that would be of value to them. My message was simple. I told them that after hanging out at their convention for a day and a half, I had heard nothing but talk about the technical aspects of web sites, and that I felt they were missing the point. A web site doesn't exist for its own sake. A web site exists to attract and keep customers. A web site exists to be of service to customers.

I told the audience of about 500 that I wished we could take a field trip through the mall down the street and observe examples of good and bad service in the stores. See what made customers happy and what frustrated them. Find out why people spent more money in one store than they did in a competing store. Then we'd bring the lessons learned back to our meeting and apply them to the design and functionality of web sites. I told them that I thought they were too swept up in how cool the Internet was, but seemed to have no grasp of what the point of the Internet should be, which it to attract and keep customers.

The group's online newsletter the next month gave this capsule review of my speech: "After attending earlier conference sessions, Calloway sensed that online newspapers have yet to really figure out what their primary goal is. Calloway gave the newspaper industry a crash course in branding."

The Internet is a most magnificent tool. I do business on it all the time. But it's not the point. Making the customer happy is the point. The New Basic is that the basic rules of business haven't changed because of the Internet. The way we deliver on those basic rules has changed, and it's created incredible opportunity for those who can stay focused on the customer.

5

Case Study: W Hotels

Making My World a Better Place

I travel all the time. The nature of my work is that I take a plane to the "office" like others drive their car every day. Most of the time I stay in the same hotel as the convention group with which I'm working. Luckily, much of this work takes place at resorts and top-flight hotels, so it's generally a pretty cushy job in terms of my accommodations.

When I have a choice, though, I default to one brand—W Hotels. If there's a W Hotel anywhere near my work, that's where I want to stay. In 2003, the annual convention of the National Speakers Association, of which I am a member, met in New Orleans in a perfectly nice chain hotel. This hotel was where all convention activities would take place and where the 1,500 attendees would be staying.

I stayed at a W Hotel two blocks away. Why? I certainly had nothing against the convention hotel. It's perfectly acceptable.

But for a five-night stay, acceptable wasn't enough for me. I wanted my room and hotel experience to be great.

As I write this, I am doing business in New York City, and since I had a choice of hotels I stayed at the W Hotel Times Square. There were probably two dozen good hotels located closer to my client, but the 10-block walk was easily worth it to me.

So what's up with W Hotels? Why have they become indispensable to me? Like almost any other indispensable choice, it's a combination of things, but in a word, W Hotels are cool. Very cool. There is a vibe and a feeling there created by a purposeful combination of sensory and service initiatives that, for me, results in a great outcome. The outcome is that my hotel stay is as positive as any other aspect of the trip, and I simply feel better in every way because of it. This makes me more effective at my work, puts me in a better mood, and makes my world a better place. Like Disney's "Make People Happy" approach, I am hard pressed to think of any business anywhere that wouldn't do well by adopting "making the customer's world a better place" as it's driving vision. From a children's day-care center to a concrete pipe manufacturer, the point is to find your version of making your customer's world a better place. This isn't touchy feely stuff. This is bottom line stuff.

Is this starting to sound like a commercial for W Hotels? That's exactly the point. That's what happens when a business becomes indispensable to customers. You create hundreds or thousands of walking commercials, which is infinitely more powerful than a full-page ad in any publication anywhere on the planet.

What Can I Learn?

What can I learn from W Hotels? Know who you are; know who your target customers are; know what they want; and know how to give it to them. You may not be a potential customer for the unique experience that W Hotels creates. You might hate spending the night there. That's not the point. The point is what any of us can learn from how W Hotels wins and keeps loyal customers.

You're a Customer—What Do *You* Want?

Don't make it more complicated than it is. You're a customer. What do *you* want? Use that as a guide to building your own company's customer experience. Barry Sternlicht, the CEO of Starwood, parent company of W Hotels, trusted his personal opinion about what would make a hotel great. Sternlicht wanted a great bed, a big TV, good water pressure, hip music everywhere, art, flowers, a cool bar, and excellent service. And he wanted it all within the context of a cutting edge vibe that virtually reeked of "cool."

You Might Be Wrong—Do It

What Sternlicht wants in a hotel might be at the opposite end of the spectrum from what you want in a hotel. But don't lose the lesson from Sternlicht's strategy. Sometimes you have to give as much credence to your own opinion as you do to the opinions of others. My friend Jo Cavender taught me that, and it's a lesson that's not always easy to implement. It takes courage. Why? Because you might be wrong. Then it's back to the drawing board.

But courage is a requirement for becoming indispensable in today's marketplace, and a big part of that courage is in being true to your vision and not giving in to the temptation to water things down in the interest of being all things to all people. You can't pull that off. Nobody can be all things to all people. And that watering down of your spicy concept will make it very unlikely that you'll ever be indispensable to anybody.

What I learn from W Hotels that applies to my business and equally applies to yours is that I can't freeze because I'm not sure that my idea will work. There's a good chance it won't. So what? That's the nature of the game. Do it anyway.

Everything Working for the Vibe

Another lesson for any business from W Hotels is that it's all about the vibe. Does your company sell replacement toner cartridges? There's a vibe around doing business with you, and it's why you are winning or losing. Do you provide marketing services to oncology clinics? Ditto. It's all about the vibe. Likewise if you are a car dealer, a ballet school, a butcher, a baker, or a candlestick maker. You're in the vibe business.

"Vibe" is what it's like to do business with you. And that's what makes you either a commodity or indispensable. In midtown Manhattan, I've got dozens of choices if all I'm looking for is a hotel room. But almost everyone is looking for a vibe. Your vibe might be functional and low key. It might be a need for great conference rooms and top-flight business services provided by no-nonsense professionals. It might be Four Seasons or Trump International luxury. It might be for a cozy bar, or a four-star restaurant, or a view of Central Park. It's all vibe.

My vibe of choice is "cool." The way Sternlicht's vision delivers cool is through a magical combination of carefully orchestrated sensory elements. The lesson for me in my strictly business-to-business company is to look at my own combination of deliverables, sensory or otherwise, and see if it creates an outcome for my customers that makes me indispensable.

Equals Cool

Here's what Sternlicht and his team have used to design an experience that, for me, equals cool. It began with an overall vision of making the hotel stay experience a sensory pleasure. Virtually everything at a W Hotel impacts one or more of your senses. For people like me, who are creatively fed, inspired, and motivated by sensory stimulation, it's the deal.

The first impression at W Hotel is often a doorman dressed, naturally, in black from head to toe, with an earpiece for instant communication discreetly in place. Enter the elevator or the lobby, and there's music. Music is everywhere. Repetitive, rhythmic, often electronic—the kind of music that either sets your perfect vibe or makes you run for something a little more traditional. Or silence, for that matter. The great majority of hotel customers would probably prefer no music at all in the common areas. Fine. W Hotels isn't after the great majority. They're after me.

For the visually hungry, like me, there are straight lines, ultra-modern minimalist styling, and art. Art is everywhere. So are flowers. In fact, the flowers are an important element in the overall art design. Perhaps the visual element with the most impact is the staff and the other guests. While my own appearance in a W Hotel does little to increase the visual cool factor, I find that staying there makes me pay more attention to what I wear. Not because I feel a need to keep up or be as cool as the twenty-something's gathered at the lobby bar. But because it's inspiring to be around an eclectic blend of personal styles.

Speaking of the lobby, often in a W Hotel the lobby bar area is adjacent to the reception desk. At W Hotel, they call this bar the "living room." The idea is to bring both locals and guests together in a place that is equally comfortable for a party of 10 friends out on the town or a lone hotel guest who simply wants to be around other people.

Let me take a break from this hotel tour to remind you of the point, which is to find the lesson for your business. What's your version of what W Hotels is doing? Not that your vibe is "cool." Your vibe might be to create a feeling of utter professionalism.

You might want to be known in your industry as being the easiest vendor with which to do business. Or the vendor who always finds the most economical solution for clients. The lesson is that every element of how you do business is either contributing to or taking away from that vibe.

Like W Hotels, let everything you do, from people to logo to product to service, be a conscious, well-thought-out decision. Don't let your vibe be one that you didn't intend. Or, just as bad, don't let it be a blank. When people ask what you're like to do business with, be sure your customers are answering, not with the same words, but with a clearly formed, compelling description of why they find you to be indispensable.

Back to the Tour—Back to the Lesson

Enter your room at a W Hotel, and plop down on the bed. My gosh, those beds! It's a combination of goose-down duvet, feather bed, and mattress. The beds are so incredibly popular that you can order one for your home. By the way, you can take many W Hotel touches home with you from the W Store in the lobby.

There's a fascinating home interior design movement in this country that is based on making your home feel as great as a cool hotel. For most people, this is nuts. Why would you want your home to be like a hotel? Because for many people, the hotel, like a W Hotel, is cool, comfortable, and provides an environment conducive to living the way they want to live. Different strokes for different folks. The lesson for my business? I want to be sure I know what my customers want, and I want to give it to them in a way that my competition can't equal.

In your room there's a CD player and CD ready to play. It's a compilation CD made just for W. Every selection is there in the interest of furthering the vibe. I almost always put the CD in immediately upon entering the room. It gets my creative energy going, and I am in the business of creating ideas. But then, who isn't?

When it's time to eat, W Hotel gives you a great restaurant on-site. Often the restaurants at W Hotels are among the most

critically acclaimed in their city. What I learn from this is that
customers, once they like doing business with you, want to buy
as much from you as they can. For a bank, this would be cross
selling of services, from loans to asset management. My version
of having a great restaurant in the hotel is being able to provide
a consulting client with a great book for each of her employees.
Get the customers in, win them over with your core product or
service, and then go deep. People want to buy more from any
business they consider to be indispensable.

Consistent Performance

W Hotels is one of the very few businesses that I feel uses product equally with people to become indispensable. But the fact remains that if the people and service aspects of the experience were
below par, it wouldn't work. My own experience is that no personal interaction at W Hotels stands out in my mind. And that's
absolutely fine. The W Hotel employees I've dealt with are subtle, professional, appropriately friendly, and, always cool. Not
cool in any sort of snobby way, but cool in a very low-key, ap-
proachable way.

What I admire about the people side of W Hotels is their
consistency. Somebody's paying attention to standards here. I
have a feeling that leadership talks a lot about who they are and
what that means in terms of customer interactions and service.
This is obviously a company that understands that company culture is vitally important to becoming indispensable to customers.
A great cultural tip-off to me is to see how the housekeeping
staff interacts with guests.

In my most recent stay at the W Hotel Times Square, I must
have entered and left my room a dozen times during the time I
was there. Not once, upon encountering a housekeeping staff
member in the hall, did that employee fail to greet me with a
genuinely friendly "hello" or "how are you today?" What made

the exchange memorable was that there was no sense of the employee having been "trained" to do this. It was very natural. My own guess is that they hire people who like people. Not just for the front desk or the restaurant wait staff, but throughout the organization.

That's What Everybody Says

On my taxi ride to LaGuardia Airport from the W Hotel Times Square, the taxi driver asked, "How do you like that hotel, the W?" My reply was, "I like it a lot. I stay there every chance I get." He said, "That's what almost everybody says that I pick up from there." Bingo. Indispensable.

It doesn't matter if you are a fan of W Hotels or not. For you it might be Marriott or Ritz-Carlton or even Days Inn. Remember the lesson. What is W Hotels doing that I need to be doing in my business? Even though their target customer and their business may be totally different from mine, what is my version of what they're doing to become indispensable?

What Is Your Uniqueness?

My friend, the author and speaker Larry Winget, is like a broken record. He repeats the same question over and over. You can't have a conversation about business with Larry without his asking, at some point, "What is your uniqueness?" Unique is the baseline differentiator. Unique isn't the safe choice. Unique breaks rules. Unique does not seek to make everyone a customer. Unique targets a particular market. And unique rules the day.

There are a lot of lessons I can learn from W Hotels, but the market value of being unique may be the most important. They are a bit like Tractor Supply Company, where they say that you can find anything they sell somewhere else, but you can't find *everything* they sell *anywhere* else. In other words, they've created a unique product mix that has powerful appeal to their target market.

By the way, it's not just me who thinks that W Hotels stand out. The readers of *Travel Savvy* magazine voted W Hotels the "Most Innovative Hotel Chain" for "proving that instead of being just another cookie-cutout, chains can be an eclectic wonderland."

What is your unique market proposition? How have you combined a package of products or services in such a way that it becomes a magnet that pulls customers right past your competition into your door? What do you do that compels your customers to see you as an utter, complete, absolute necessity?

I Can't Get It Anywhere Else

Did you ever notice that the most powerful competitive concepts are truly the simplest? Think of any business that you consider indispensable. I can almost guarantee that the baseline reason you see them as being a necessity is because, whatever it is they make, sell, or do, you simply can't get it anywhere else. You might find the product, but not the people. Someone else might duplicate or exceed their service, but not the location. Ten competitors may beat them on price, but not the combination of what they offer.

Can you truthfully say that you have something that customers can't get anywhere else? If you can, and there's a demand for it, then you're onto something. If you can, but there's no demand for it, then you've got a hobby, and you need to find something else that can be your business. If you can't, then you have to go back to the drawing board and get creative.

6

Create
Community

Los Lobos

I was waiting at the gate for the LaGuardia to Nashville flight when I noticed a group of guys wander into the area and take seats, obviously waiting for the same flight. Something told me I knew them somehow. Bingo. Los Lobos. The East Los Angeles band best known for their hit song "La Bamba." Which is a shame. That song's not a great representation of the amazing music that this band plays. Los Lobos makes music the likes of which no other band anywhere on this planet or any other can equal in terms of pure heart, soul, and rock and roll pleasure.

I immediately called up my friend Kris Young in Minneapolis. Kris works for the event production company Martin Bastian, and she has worked with Los Lobos on a few occasions. She's a friend and fan of the band. I left her a message that I knew would bring her absolute delight, as she and I, besides being great friends, share that Los Lobos bond.

On the plane, as the band members filed past to take their seats, I just looked up at them and said, "Best band in the world." Smiles broke out among the guys along with a couple of, "Hey, thank you, man," greetings from the band. It made my day.

The next day, at a party at Ruckus Film, a film production company in Nashville, I told my friend, film director Coke Sams, about my Los Lobos encounter. "One of the best concerts I ever went to in my life was Los Lobos at 328 Performance Hall about 10 years ago. They just totally rocked the place," Coke said. We went on to discuss the finer points of the music of Los Lobos, and others entered the conversation, expressing either equal enthusiasm about the band, or saying they really weren't that familiar with them and wanting to know more about why we were such big fans.

What does this have to do with your business becoming indispensable? The second that Los Lobos' new CD, "Let's Ride," was released, I bought a copy. Just like I bought a copy the second their previous CD was released. You get the picture. This is a brand that compels customer loyalty.

It goes beyond their music. It gets to one of the most powerful customer loyalty factors in the marketplace: community. You're not just a lone Los Lobos fan. You're a member of the Los Lobos community of fans. It's a community made even more special to us because not that many people "get it." As one who appreciates the music of Los Lobos, you are a breed apart. You know just a little more about great music. You're a cut above the average mass pop music fan.

I'm presenting a tongue in cheek description of a snobby community of rock and roll connoisseurs, and yet there's an element of important truth there. We Los Lobos fans are in on what may be the best-kept secret in popular music, and we like being members of that particular club.

The Power of Community

The Driver of continuous connection is largely about creating community. If you get community built around your business, your product, or your service, you've tapped into the mother lode of pure marketing power. The product that may best leverage the power of community is Apple, maker of the iPod. I know that when I'm sitting on a plane listening to my iPod, any other iPod user that spots me will give me an almost imperceptible nod of recognition. And in that moment of shared product community, our loyalty to the brand just became a little bit stronger.

The Harley riders or Porsche drivers who wave to each other as they pass on the highway have shared product community. Notice that their waves are understated, not any big hand up in the air waving wildly with big grin recognition of a fellow brand traveler. It's subtle. It's cool. It's a bond that says even though I may be a free-spirited, long-haired, tattooed, bad-to-the-bone Harley guy, and you are a short-haired, wingtip-wearing-during-the-week dentist out for your usual weekend born-to-be-wild Harley fantasy, we share something significant. We bought the same stuff. As the Harley riders would say, "If I have to explain it, you wouldn't understand."

Where's the lesson for me? As I work to position my little company as being a complete and absolute necessity with my corporate clients, what can I learn from Los Lobos or iPod? I'd better learn that the more community I can build around the brand called Joe Calloway, the more competitive I become. Ditto for your company. There's an old African saying that we return to old watering holes for more than water. We return because friends and dreams are there to meet us.

I Like You Because You're Like Me

Many of Starbucks' most loyal customers don't like coffee and never drink coffee. They go to Starbucks because other people like them go to Starbucks. They sit in their favorite chairs at their favorite tables and hang out with their friends who also don't like coffee but adore the chai lattes. These are individuals who may like all different kinds of people, but sometimes like to be with people who are like themselves in many ways. It's a comfort zone. It's a place to belong. Starbucks isn't selling coffee to them. Starbucks is selling community. At the same time, they're using the Driver of engage, enchant, and enthrall.

The people who are most enthusiastic about the presentations I make to business conventions aren't always the ones who take the most pure information or competitive ideas away from the experience. It's often the ones who relate in a very powerful and personal way to one or more of the stories that I told to illustrate a point. They think, "Hey, that same thing has happened to ME!" This shared experience creates an immediate bond between them and me, and we've got community happening. That strengthens my market position.

It becomes even more powerful when they discover others in the audience who had the same feeling. Then they start sharing their own stories about similar experiences and feelings and even more community results. When they credit Joe Calloway as being the source of that community, and want to experience it again, then I move toward becoming indispensable.

Can Any Business Create Community?

Short answer: Yes. Longer answer: Yes, and your challenge is to figure out how instead of taking the losing position of thinking that community doesn't apply to you. Baloney. It doesn't apply only if you choose to ignore the loyalty-building potential you have to create community. There are an infinite number of ways that you can bring people together around your product or business. The car dealer that has monthly "Understanding Your Car" seminars with free hot dogs and barbeque for new owners is the car dealer that understands the power of community. The dry cleaner that sponsors a local Little League team and shows up for every game to sit with the parents of the players understands community. The restaurant that posts its most popular recipes and gives constantly updated tips on food and wine on its web site totally gets the concept of community.

Sex and the City

What made HBO's television series *Sex and the City* one of the hottest brands in television history? Community. The show was not only about the community of four women living in New York City, it created community among women, and, to a lesser extent men, who were raving fans of this show that they considered to be an utter, complete, absolute necessity. I only wish that my customers were as devoted to doing business with me as *Sex and the City* fans were to doing business with it.

The day after each new *Sex and the City* episode was shown, the country almost literally buzzed with the phone calls, lunch conversations, and hallway talk about what had happened on the show. It's continuous connection and it's being able to engage, enchant, and enthrall. One good gal pal of mine confessed to being a raving fan who simply had to see the program each week. She said that the big draw to her and her friends was that the characters talked about the same things that women talk about in real life. In other words, the feeling was that these characters are "like us."

What lesson do I learn from *Sex and the City*? Probably the most useful is that I want my clients to feel that I "get them." That I know who they are and what they're about and what makes them tick. When a bank tells me that I can "speak their language," it's no different than the *Sex and the City* characters speaking the language of the millions of women who watched every week. I have always said that if I could have any single competitive advantage it would be to know and understand more about the customer than anyone else. *Sex and the City*, with its target market, did exactly that.

Shared Experiences—Good and Bad

Over the past 20 years, I have done a tremendous amount of work with what are commonly known as users groups. An example would be a users group made up of companies who all use the same brand of computers. I've worked with lots of high-tech users groups like NEAX Users, IBM Users, CIS Users, the NEAX 2400 IMS Users Group, the IBX Users Group, and the list goes on and on. The whole point of a users group is to create community that helps each member make better use of this product with which they have a shared experience. And this, in turn, strengthens the manufacturer's bond with the customers, provided, of course, that there is a high level of responsiveness to the needs of the members of the group. Do your own version of a users group with your customers. Get your customers together in one room, and let them build loyalty to you through their shared experiences. This kind of discussion serves to create and sustain momentum around your product. This presupposes, of course, that their shared experiences are positive ones, or that you can immediately bring solutions to the negative ones.

Sometimes community is formed around shared experiences that some might characterize as "bad" ones. One of Amazon.com's innovations was to invite customers to post their opinions about products right on the purchase page. Look at the order page for one of my books, and you will see reviews by customers. These reviews include the good, the bad, and the ugly, although I've been fortunate enough not to have too many that fit into the latter categories. A poor review of a particular product may not serve to sell that product, but it certainly strengthens the community bond between Amazon's customers, and that in turn serves to build loyalty to Amazon itself. It's truly a big picture outcome embraced by Amazon that goes far beyond product, price, and service.

We Are What We Buy

It may be a bad thing. It may be a good thing. But the fact is that, to a certain degree, we are what we buy. You can discover much about what a person is really like by simply knowing what he or she buys. This means that products and services have become much more than functional in nature. They are cultural.

If you tell me that you drink Pepsi Cola, drive a Monte Carlo, wear clothes from The Gap, love NASCAR, listen to Brooks and Dunn, eat at Outback Steakhouse, and vacation every year in Destin, Florida, that all adds up to a particular picture of who you are. If, on the other hand, you tell me that you drink Red Bull, drive an Audi, wear clothes from Brooks Brothers, love pro tennis, listen to Branford Marsalis, eat at The Palm, and vacation every year in Aspen, it paints quite a different picture.

Don't miss the point here. What's important is that whatever you are selling needs to connect with your customer on a culturally defining level. If your customers are business buyers, the principal remains the same. You must be part of the community that helps define that corporate or industrial customer's image of who they are and what they value. That's what every one of those brands named above have in common. They all help customers define their image of who they are.

My customers are companies who want to work with experts who can help them grow their businesses. This is true right down to the vendors they use to clean their buildings or provide them with in-house copying services. My customers are not companies who are looking for the lowest cost provider in everything they buy. Your customers may be purely "lowest price buyers." If so, you have my condolences. And for those of you who are saying, "Well, my customers really DO only buy on price. What can I do?" Uh, you have to have the lowest price. If what you are saying is literally true, and your customers buy only on price, then you either have to have the lowest price or you must find another line of work. Sorry. End of story. Of course, the truth is that your customers almost certainly aren't buying only on price. You just think they are.

Stop Advertising and Start Hanging Out

How can you create more community with your existing and potential customers? You might consider pulling back on your advertising and spending some of that money on interactive, face-to-face, experiential marketing. There are a variety of ways to do this. The idea is to connect with your market in ways that let you create a real-time experience. For an incredible example of building community and becoming indispensable, read about Deluxe Financial Services, Inc. in the case study in this book.

Standing in front of a group doing a live presentation can be one of the most effective ways to sell your company and build community. Send your best people out to talk about either your company specifically, or your industry, to groups that include potential customers. If you're good in the front of a room talking about what you do and how you do it, the positive effect can be enormous. Minimize the use of PowerPoint, by the way. Better yet, leave it at home. The person who can make a presentation by just standing up and talking intelligently and entertainingly about what he does is worth his weight in gold to any company wanting to create community.

Make your web site so compelling that it finds a place on the computer "favorites" list of web sites of your target market. Do it by giving away information that helps your customers do something better, grow their own business, or just have fun with whatever you offer to them on the site.

Make product launches, personnel additions or promotions, new service initiatives, or virtually anything else you do a reason to throw a party. Don't just take out an ad or send a press release. Have an event.

Bring your customers together for seminars that can help them grow their businesses. Or, if you are in the consumer market, bring them together to experience anything that will put you in a favorable light with them, whether it's directly related to your product or not. No matter who your customer is, you can figure out a way to have live bodies mingling face to face in a way that creates community for you.

My friend Robin Crow owns a recording studio that hosts a barbeque every Friday throughout the summer months each year. It's simply a way to bring clients, friends, and influencers together in a way that creates a positive, ongoing buzz about Dark Horse Recording Studio. You may be thinking that this sort of thing just isn't done in your business. Duh! That's the point! Be the first! It wasn't done in Robin's business either until he started doing it.

The Heart of Business

This is all about heart. It's about how much heart you have built in to your company's culture, and it's about your ability to touch the hearts of your customers. Think that heart doesn't really matter in your business? Well, answer this question: Do you want your customers to love doing business with you? If the answer is yes, then rest assured that you're talking about heart.

Most business people tend to shy away from topics like heart and community. They just want to know how to grow market share. Fine. You grow market share through heart and community. A few years ago, I had a young entrepreneur tell me that this heart and community stuff was all well and good, but that in his business the name of the game was generation of revenue. I just laughed and walked away. There was no hope of getting him to see that revenue is generated and sustained by creating customers who love you. He didn't get it. He wasn't going to get it. My guess is that his business folded long ago.

An Inside Job

The most important community is the one within your organization. If there's no sense of belonging there, then you don't have a snowball's chance in hell of creating community with customers. If working in your company isn't fun and fulfilling and an overall positive experience, then doing business with you won't be either. You might last or even do fairly well for a while, but over the long haul, without community within the organization, you're toast. You'll also be completely unable to create and sustain momentum.

It almost gets ridiculous for someone to ask how to build community within an organization. Countless books have been written on just that subject, but for Pete's sake, let's bottom line it. You build community within an organization by treating people with respect. Follow that rule. Just treat people with respect, which I believe includes listening, appreciating, trusting, and telling each other the truth. I'd say that's about as complicated as it needs to be.

7

Case Study: Gitomer

Gitomer Rocks

In the world in which I live—consulting, training, writing, and speaking—Jeffrey Gitomer is an original. He's a sensation. His organization is the envy of others in the industry. In short, Gitomer and his crew absolutely rock. They are masters of the Five Drivers.

Jeffrey Gitomer is the author of the *New York Times* bestseller *The Sales Bible*. He also wrote *Customer Satisfaction Is Worthless: Customer Loyalty Is Priceless, The Patterson Principles of Selling,* and his latest book, *The Little Red Book of Selling.* Jeffrey's books have sold more than 500,000 copies worldwide.

Jeffrey delivers seminars, runs annual sales meetings, and conducts training programs on selling and customer loyalty. He has presented an average of 120 seminars a year for the past 10 years. Jeffrey's customers include Coca-Cola, Caterpillar, BMW, Cingular Wireless, Hilton, Enterprise Rent-A-Car, Comcast Cable,

Time Warner Cable, Wells Fargo Bank, Blue Cross Blue Shield, Hyatt Hotels, Carlsburg Beer, Wausau Insurance, Glaxo-SmithKline, IBM, AT&T, and hundreds of others.

His syndicated column *Sales Moves* appears in more than 95 business newspapers and is read by more than four million people every week. Jeffrey is the host of *Selling Power Live* audio magazine, distributed to over 10,000 subscribers worldwide. His three web sites—www.gitomer.com, www.trainone.com, and www.knowsuccess.com—get as many as 5,000 hits a day from readers and seminar attendees. His state-of-the-art web-presence and e-commerce ability have set the standard among peers and has won huge praise and acceptance from customers. A weekly, streaming-video sales training lesson is available on www.trainone.com. The content is fun, pragmatic, real world, and immediately implementable. Gitomer and his innovative team are leading the way in the field of e-learning.

Create Value, Then Give It Away

I went to Charlotte, North Carolina, to hang out with Gitomer and crew and see if I could discover some of the rocket science that's resulted in their incredible success. Alas, no rocket science. It turns out that Jeffrey's not that much different from the other extraordinary performers in business. Jeffrey does those obvious things (the Five Drivers) that his competition simply won't do. Most of what Jeffrey does is available to anyone willing to flip the switch and do the work.

In a session designed to let me pick Jeffrey's amazing brain, while he juggled phone calls, staff interactions, video tapings for his online training, decisions on advertising for future seminars, and about seven thousand other activities, I got to the key factor that makes Gitomer so successful. I asked Jeffrey to tell me what's at the heart of his whole operation. There was absolute certainty in the way he answered. No hesitation. No beating around the bush. "Create value, then give it away. If you have good stuff, people want more," Jeffrey replied.

You're possibly thinking, "This is another one of those ideas that sounds peachy in a book but in the real world it won't work. You don't make money giving away your product." Sure you do. But the catch is that your product has to deliver value. If you think that giving away value doesn't work, then turn on your radio.

Jeffrey followed up on his own statement by illustrating it with an example from the music business. Exhibit A: The Rolling Stones give their music away on the radio. Customers hear it for free. Rolling Stones customers perceive value in that music to the point of going into record stores, buying CDs, and paying up to $1,000 a ticket for front row seats at concerts. Don't even start to think that giving away value doesn't work. It not only works, it can make you indispensable and make you a fortune at the same time.

Exhibit B: Mrs. Fields Cookies. Debbie Fields says that whenever she would open a new store the standard operating procedure was to give the cookies away. People like the cookies. People then buy the cookies. Give away value. If you have a great product, you not only have nothing to fear in giving it away, you're crazy not to.

Both the Rolling Stones and Mrs. Fields are able to engage, enchant, and enthrall their customers with their products and everything that surrounds them. Jeffrey does much the same thing. He creates magic by often flying in the face of what is traditionally done and said in his field, and hooking in customers with the power of his own uniqueness. As Jeffrey puts it, "All we do as a result of giving away chunks of my stuff is create fans and make money." Give away value. They want more. Wow, what a concept.

Jeffrey gives away his ideas to about four million people a week in his column on sales. Here's the key: It creates a vacuum. People read it and want more. So they buy his books, sign up for his e-zine, attend his seminars. Speaking of buying his books, the very day that I was in Jeffrey's office he had four books in the Amazon top 20, including three in the top 10, one of which was his *Little Red Book of Selling* at number one. These numbers aren't just impressive. They're gaudy. If you ever wanted to see the concept of becoming indispensable clearly illustrated, this is it. If Jeffrey writes it, his customers will buy it. They can't live without it. Gitomer doesn't just have customers. He has fans— raving fans.

Jeffrey explains a lot of this dynamic as the law of attraction. "People want to be with people they identify with," Jeffrey says. Clearly Jeffrey is a street-smart sales guy who shoots as straight with people as anyone I've ever known. There's no fluff in what Jeffrey is selling, just the red meat kind of stuff that his customers hunger for constantly. If he failed to deliver on this value, he'd be out of business. Jeffrey and team have been able to develop habitual dependability as a major characteristic of their business.

A great builder of community within his customer base, Jeffrey does continuous connection as well as anyone on the planet. Much of his staff's effort is devoted to this Driver. He creates community by staying in touch, and his customers create new business for Jeffrey at the same time by constantly talking about him and his products. Jeffrey's e-zine went from 20,000 subscribers to close to 100,000 in two years because his customers told people about it.

They Don't Do What I Do

Jeffrey Gitomer operates in a market that is literally packed with competitors. There's a sales trainer on every corner, and the number of books and tapes on selling seems to get bigger every year. It would appear that the whole subject of teaching people how to sell has become a commodity.

I asked Jeffrey what he thought set him apart from the other sales trainers. "They don't do what I do. They teach people how to sell." Jeffrey said. "I don't teach that. I teach why people buy. That's a much more powerful thing to understand. But the main thing is that I teach putting value first. Value first is based on the premise that people don't like to be sold but they love to buy," he said. This is called taking a big picture outcome view of what you do. I asked Jeffrey if he used that philosophy with his own products. "We create opportunities to buy and watch the sparks fly," he said.

Jeffrey's not a shy, retiring type when it comes to talking about what differentiates him. "I'm the best salesman in the world. I believe that in my heart. But I don't sell. I create value and give people the opportunity to buy." Jeffrey believes that there are three keys in creating a successful sales business, or any other endeavor, for that matter. "First is value," he said. "Then you have to understand that people love to buy. And, finally, you've got to understand that in sales, it's not who you know, it's who knows you." This gets back to Jeffrey's mastery of continuous connection. He connects with and is famous in an entire market because of the differentiated position to which he aspires.

The World-Class Expert

Jeffrey doesn't want to be a guy who comes to mind when you think of sales training. Jeffrey wants to be THE guy. Period. "There are three levels of expert," Jeffrey says. "There's being an Expert. There's being a World-Class Expert. And there's being THE World-Class Expert." Jeffrey claims the latter title. This wouldn't mean that much if he were the only one saying it. But

I've always believed that the market decides. And a very, very big chunk of the market has decided that Jeffrey is THE guy.

A big, big part of Jeffrey's success is a result of bringing together a team of people who are extraordinary in their own right. This is where Jeffrey's ability to create and sustain momentum becomes the fuel that drives this remarkable machine. I asked Jeffrey to talk about what makes his people so effective.

"I let them achieve for themselves, not just for me. I encourage them to take risks," Jeffrey said. "They can make mistakes and be rewarded. In our company if you screw something up you get $100 cash. Believe me, they didn't screw it up on purpose, and I don't want them to feel penalized for taking a risk. People won't take a risk if they fear reprisal. My reprisal is to give them $100. Sometimes when they screw up I'm so upset I can't stand it. But can you imagine your boss yelling at you and handing you $100 cash at the same time? That's not a bad deal," Jeffrey said.

The Web Mistress and the Queen of Events

Traci Capraro and Michelle Joyce are Jeffrey's two longest tenured employees and key players in his organization. While the product is Jeffrey and his ideas, the reason it all works so well is employees like Traci and Michelle. At Gitomer, they not only have fun with the work and each other, they get to have fun with their official titles.

Traci is the Web Mistress and Director of Media. Her responsibilities include public relations, weekly column distribution, procurement of new journals, billing, and radio, television, and print interviews. Her marketing duties include new book press kits and mailings. Traci is also the editor and list manager of their weekly e-mail magazine *Sales Caffeine*. She manages and promotes quarterly teleseminars, manages and updates the web site, as well as handling customer online support. More than anyone, Traci is probably the key player in establishing and maintaining a continuous connection with customers. This is the lifeblood of the Gitomer success formula.

Michelle is the Queen of Events. Her responsibilities include qualifying corporate seminar leads and finding the right solutions for customers. Gitomer offers a variety of training solutions ranging from personalized seminars to training products. Michelle's job is to find the best fit for each client to ensure the most productive results. She participates in Jeffrey's conference calls and meetings with clients. She takes an active role on each conference call, capturing thoughts and ideas that help personalize each seminar. It's about seeing that big picture outcome. The ultimate point of Michelle's job is creating memorable seminar experiences for clients, so they want to do more business with Gitomer. It's about being able to engage, enchant, and enthrall.

Not wanting to just take Jeffrey's word on why his team works so well, and how he and they are able to create and sustain momentum, I asked Michelle Joyce and Traci Capraro to share some thoughts about how they do what they do so remarkably well. As you read their comments, look for the Five Drivers running through everything that they say.

Calloway: Tell me how being able to take a risk, make mistakes, and get $100 for screwing up empowers you. How does it help the business succeed?

Joyce: From my very first day on the job, Jeffrey has always told me that I cannot fail. He has always empowered me to take risks, try new approaches, and find my own way. It's so encouraging to work for someone who truly believes in you and supports your decisions.

Capraro: The first mistake I ever made was during the first week on the job. I arranged a live radio interview for a Saturday afternoon and forgot to tell Jeffrey about it. When the interviewer called me on Monday morning to inform me that Jeffrey missed the interview, I was devastated. Not only did I put the radio station in a terrible situation, but I made Jeffrey look bad. Jeffrey made light of the situation and gave me a $100 bill (as I cried in his office, afraid I was going to lose my job). He said if I didn't screw up, I wasn't trying hard enough. That was my formal invitation to try harder.

Joyce: Jeffrey is my mentor. I learn from him, and he teaches me how to learn from my own mistakes. He encourages others to keep learning, keep growing, and to step outside of their comfort zones. Sure, you will experience growing pains, but they only make you stronger.

Capraro: I'm generally not a risk taker. But since I've met Jeffrey, I've taken more risks in my professional career than I've taken in my personal life. What's the worst that can happen? I earn $100 bucks? So I've sent e-mails out when I shouldn't have; I've created marketing materials without approval; and I've done some pretty risky things. Some have worked like a charm, some have not. But both my company and I have learned from every risk. I have personally grown in some way with every risk. If I had worried every time about losing my job from taking a risk, I wouldn't be where I am today and neither would our company.

Calloway: This is Jeffrey's company. In a sense, it's all about Jeffrey. So why do you and the other employees have such enthusiasm for and commitment to the company?

Capraro: Why am I enthusiastic about this company? I believe in my product. I believe in our training. I believe in our company. I think we're the best sales training firm in the world, and I believe I work for the best sales trainer in the world. Who wouldn't be enthusiastic about that? And I'm fortunate to work in an environment where my coworkers feel the same. We're all here because we love our company, and we'll do whatever it takes to make it the best.

Joyce: Jeffrey is an amazing individual. He is dedicated to his work and to helping others, and has a truly genuine spirit. By empowering his employees, he sets a standard of hard work, dedication, and pride in our company. He shares his success with each of us, and we believe in him. Jeffrey runs the company like a family and, in a sense, we all want to make our "dad" proud.

Jeffrey believes in taking care of his "family." He provides every employee with paid health insurance, gym memberships, store memberships, AAA memberships, and legal services (so that they are healthy, fed, and safe). We have staff dinners, celebrate birthdays and holidays, and take trips together. He has created an environment of people who work hard together and play hard together, and who never want that enthusiasm to end.

Calloway: Why are so many of your customers raving fans who buy everything you put in front of them?

Joyce: The very foundation of our company is to provide memorable service. More importantly, we provide value first. We have not created a company that sells products and services. We have created a company that is willing to help anyone and offer the best solution. Customers will test us—we welcome it. Every employee follows Jeffrey's principle of "recover, plus one." We don't just solve a problem; we take it to the next level to create a positive experience for everyone. Every customer is treated like they are the most important person in the world . . . from the big name seminar client to the individual sales beginner.

Capraro: Our clients are so enthusiastic because we give them value at the outset. Jeffrey's column appears in 95 newspapers weekly. Our e-zine is circulated to tens of thousands of people every week. All are free. We are constantly staying in front of our customers and prospects with something that they can learn from—something that they see as valuable. When they are ready to buy, we're right there staring them in the face.

When we ask them to buy, they've been getting our information for free for so long, they almost feel like they have to buy.

Calloway: If there's one thing that you feel is your own personal strength in making Gitomer customers loyal, what is it? In other words, do you have any kind of personal standard of performance or an outcome that you want to create with every customer?

Capraro: I think that my own personal strength is my willingness to help. Sometimes people call in and don't know what type of training they need, or why they didn't get their weekly email, or where their latest purchase is. I'll take responsibility for every call or complaint that I get. I want to see that they get their problem or question handled in the fastest and friendliest way possible. I tell them what I would want to hear if I had that question or problem. Just an honest answer from someone who cares. And if I can't help them, I refer them to someone in the office who can, then I personally follow up to make sure it is handled. If I feel that there was an error on our part, I'll send them something free. Whether it's an advertising specialty, or even a product, just the extra something really makes the customer feel special. That's what keeps them coming back.

Joyce: I have a genuine interest in helping people, and I have fun at what I do. I create a personal relationship with all of my customers, and they become my friends. I am also truly dedicated to our company and the services we offer. We are in the business of helping people. If I can't offer the best solution for you, I will help you find it somewhere else.

Calloway: Anything else you'd like to say about the "magic" that is Gitomer and company?

Joyce: The magic of our company is best defined by its people. We have a team of amazing leaders who work hard to be their best. I cannot imagine a greater place to work.

8

Obvious but Often Overlooked

Duh!

It's a never-ending source of amazement, amusement, and frustration for me to see how many people in business overlook the most obvious truths. This is kindergarten stuff like, "first impressions count," and "saying it's so doesn't make it so," and "always tell the truth." It's as if some people put on blinders when confronted with a glaring weakness in their company. This chapter is a look at some of the obvious mistakes made by companies that keep them from becoming indispensable. This is the "Duh!" stuff that is strangling thousands of companies with good products and good services that seemingly don't have a clue about how to behave sometimes. Remember: We don't get hurt by what we don't know. We get hurt by what we know but don't do.

Obvious 1: You Had Me at Hello

In the movie *Jerry Maguire* the title character, played by Tom Cruise, is looking for the right words to win the heart of Dorothy Boyd, played by Renee Zellweger. As he stammers his way through his clumsy expression of feelings, she stops him by saying, "You had me at hello." You can have your customers at hello, if you say it right. There is more and more evidence that how a customer is met in the initial contact with a company is a determining factor in whether she stays or leaves, both in the short term and long term.

This week I had lunch with a friend who works at one of the best companies I know. They do everything right, almost all the time. I say "almost all the time" because my experience with them on this occasion was just mystifying. It was one of those things where you find yourself thinking, "How can this possibly happen here?"

This is a company that prides itself on consistency of performance and on getting the details right. They are known for their friendly and helpful people, who are a big part of the essence of their brand. This company trains, retrains, and constantly communicates a handful of basic values to employees, one of which is treating customers like friends and greeting everyone in a friendly, helpful manner.

What's the Secret Password?

I walked into the lobby of the company headquarters and approached the reception desk to check in for my appointment. The woman behind the desk was making some notes about something, so I waited for her to finish. She finished. She then moved on to her next task which was to call someone and inform them that their meeting for later in the day had been cancelled. I waited for her to finish. She finished. She then moved on to her next task, which involved doing something on the computer. At this point, it began to feel almost surreal. I am standing quite literally three feet in front of her, she clearly knows I'm there, and she has obviously placed me on the lower region of her "To Do" list.

Okay. I give up. What's the secret password?

I said hello. She looked up briefly then returned her concentration to the computer. I said, "Excuse me, I'm here to meet someone." With a look of resignation because she was going to be forced to interrupt her day at the reception desk to actually receive someone, she asked, "And who are you here to see?" I gave her the name, she called him, he came down and off to lunch we went. I didn't tell him about what had happened, but I'm going to. You can't solve a problem if you don't know it exists.

But That Doesn't Happen Here

Aren't you happy that such a thing could never happen at your company? Don't be so happy. You may be thinking, "Yeah, that's terrible, but that doesn't happen here." Those sound suspiciously like famous last words to me. What indispensable companies do is assume that such a breakdown in expectations can happen at anytime, and they are constantly vigilant against such an occurrence.

Let me be the first to raise my hand and say, "Guilty as charged!" I was having dinner in the restaurant where I am a partner, and I noticed that a party of four people had been seated and water brought to their table, but no one had taken a drink order from them. They were waiting a bit longer than I considered acceptable, and that "bit longer" soon turned into a ridiculously long time with no service. I stepped in and made sure that a member of the wait staff took their order, I bought them a round of drinks on me, and generally did all the things you do to try and make amends for such a mess.

The damage had been done. We most definitely did not "have them at hello." I'm sure that they were wondering what the secret password was. The lesson for me and for you is that even though your people are trained and motivated to be responsive, there will be times that you fall short. Missing the mark at any point in the relationship with a customer is detrimental, obviously, but for it to happen as a first impression is one of the unforgivable sins in business.

Why Clichés Become Clichés

"You never get a second chance to make a first impression." Yeah, yeah, right. What a cliché. Hey, ideas become clichés because they're true. To be indispensable to your customers you have to concentrate a lot of energy around first impressions, whether they are at the front door, on the phone, or on the web site.

Do some mystery shopping around your first impressions. Hire an outside company to check you out. It may be the smartest money and time you spend this year. If you have a weak link in your pattern of first impressions, it's costing you more business than you might guess.

When asked what his favorite restaurant was, the famous chef James Beard replied, "My favorite restaurant is the one where they know me." The first impression in each customer transaction or touchpoint, even with a lifelong customer, is critical to creating or maintaining loyalty.

Obvious 2: Saying It Doesn't Make It So

Pay attention to advertising today. My vote for the most used and least truthful advertising slogan is "We Exceed Our Customers' Expectations." It's become an immensely popular phrase in corporate mission statements, company vision statements, and advertising for almost every kind of company you can think of. It's definitely the slogan of the day.

I recently read an ad for an upscale Manhattan hotel that had undergone a renovation. The ad claimed that guests' expectations would be exceeded by such amenities as high-speed Internet access, flat screen TVs, and a spacious work area. Hello! This is an upscale hotel with upscale prices. Everything they're claiming as "extras" are entry-level expectations. Wow. I bet the bathrooms come with convenient hot and cold running water, too.

It's a real knee slapper, isn't it? I hear everybody and their brother claiming that they'll exceed my expectations, and I laugh so hard I sometimes blow milk out my nose. The fact is that a very precious few companies exceed anyone's expectations. It's those companies that do that are indispensable.

When's the last time you surprised a long-time customer? That's a good indicator of whether or not you're exceeding expectations. If things are going along nicely and it's business as usual with your oldest and best customers, then it's doubtful that you're exceeding anything, except possibly the time limit on how long you'll keep those relationships intact. Right now somebody out there is figuring the means to surprise your customers in a way that will make them think, "Hey. Why didn't YOU ever do this for me?"

A Job Well Done Exceeds Nobody's Expectations

I'm a fan of the American Express card. I have three of them, two of which are for work, plus a personal card. In the interest of full disclosure, let me also note that American Express is a client of mine. The reason I'm a fan of American Express as a customer is purely and simply because of the consistency of their high level of service. When compared to their competitors, whose cards I also have, there's only one card that's indispensable to me and it's American Express.

But not even American Express is going to exceed my expectations every time on every transaction. Most of the time they simply do what I'm paying them to do. For example, I needed to track down some information about a particular charge I'd made to an airline on my American Express card. I called the 1-800 customer service number, a young woman handled my inquiry, got me the necessary information quickly and accurately, and was just as pleasant as she could be. At the end of the call she asked permission to ask a question, which I granted. She wanted to know if she had "exceeded my expectations this morning." I immediately told her that, no, she hadn't.

I could almost hear her jaw drop at the other end of the phone line. "Oh my gosh, what did I do wrong?" she asked, obviously concerned that she had made a mistake or offended me in some way. "You didn't do anything wrong." I said. "You did a great job. You did exactly what I pay American Express to do."

Let's get clear about something. You don't become indispensable by doing a good job and selling a great product. Big deal. That's minimum entry-level stuff. That's what I pay you to do. That's exactly what I expect you to do. To get to the indispensable category, you have to do something the customer considers extra-ordinary, in the literal sense of the word. Extra-ordinary: Beyond the norm. Beyond what anyone would do in the same situation.

This Is Very Cool

On the flip side, here's where American Express has exceeded my expectations. I had my credit cards stolen and duly reported the theft to all companies with whom I had cards. I called all of the companies on the same afternoon and each one assured me that they'd get replacement cards to me immediately.

Two of the companies delivered my cards to me about seven or eight days later. The very morning after I had made the calls, however, UPS delivered my new American Express cards to my office. Approximately 18 hours after I made the call, the new cards were delivered. Now this exceeded my expectations.

I know full well that the other cards were issued through banks and that there's another whole layer of logistics they must go through to get me replacement cards. I have no complaint with them. But the fact remains that American Express surprised me because there had been no discussion about expediting the replacement of the cards. They just did it.

We'll Take Care of It

A further example of American Express exceeding my expectations and, at the same time, clearly differentiating themselves from their competitors involved disputed charges to the card. I use credit cards a lot in business and travel, and there is the occasional charge that simply makes no sense to me. I can't recall making it and it doesn't look familiar in any way.

I reported one such charge on an American Express card and was told simply to not worry about it, not pay it, and they'd handle it from there. "We'll take care of it," the customer service rep told me. I never heard another thing about it. When I thought about it a few weeks later, I experienced a subtle but definite feeling of being pleasantly surprised. Expectations were being quietly exceeded.

This contrasts with my experience with another credit card company, which, when I reported a disputed charge, sent me forms to fill out and affidavits to have signed and notarized, for Pete's sake! Not good. And way below expectations, especially when compared to the standard that American Express has set.

Expectations Compared to What?

If you are my auto dealer, my dry cleaner, my accountant, the company that cleans my office building, my web site designer, my barber, my banker, my doctor, my stock broker, or anyone else with whom I do business, then you'd best understand where my expectations come from. When you claim that you'll exceed my expectations you have to ask this: Expectations compared to what? Compared to whom?

Compared to American Express, for starters. I will also compare you to every other business that delivers a higher level of product, service, or experience to me in any way whatsoever. This gets to the idea that your competition is everybody. Not just everybody else who's in a similar business to you. Everybody! Your customers compare you to anyone who sets a higher standard.

It Wasn't the Way He Wanted It

Our family moved into a new home not long ago. This house knocked me out in just about every way and did pretty much the same for my wife and our little girl. We loved this house and were happy with virtually every single thing about it. The workmanship was exceptional, and the quality was obvious throughout.

When we closed the purchase, the house was complete and ready to go. The day after closing, I happened to stop by the house and found some workmen there, working on the granite kitchen counters and making some adjustments to fixtures. When I inquired as to what was going on, one of the guys told me that Rogan (Rogan Allen, the builder of the house) had spotted a couple of things that weren't the way he wanted. He'd seen some details that weren't right. His standards hadn't quite been met.

The operative idea here is that this was the day after closing. The house was finished. There was nothing in the contract about doing any corrective work in the house. Rogan Allen, the homebuilder, had taken it upon himself to correct what he had seen as minor imperfections. Neither my wife nor I had seen a thing. We were satisfied with the house just as it was. Rogan wasn't satisfied, and he took it upon himself to make the improvements.

Rogan Allen exceeded my expectations. It cost him money to do it. And I will tell that story to a lot of people. I just did. What do you think it's worth to Rogan to have a customer like me whose expectations were exceeded? He's definitely moving toward becoming indispensable in this case. If you want to be indispensable to me, then do what Rogan did. Don't just claim in some ad or mission statement that you exceed my expectations. Make me say "Wow. I would never have expected that."

Obvious 3: Tell the Truth

Conduct your own personal truth survey over the next week. How many times do companies lie to you? I understand that my use of the word "lie" is a bold position to take. Maybe it would be nicer to ask how many times you received inaccurate information from a business. I'm going to stick with "How many times did companies lie to you?" This is a problem that is real, and yet most people pay little or no attention to the possibility that they're lying to customers every day. Moral considerations aside, lying is inefficient, it's ineffective, and it's reached epidemic proportions.

My guess is that the vast majority of people reading this book doesn't lie or ever purposely mislead customers, coworkers, or anyone else for that matter. So I'm actually addressing two audiences here. One is the majority, whom I hope will take this chapter and let it be an inspiration to help stamp out lying by the companies with whom you do business. The other is the minority. These are the liars. The ones who, as a matter of course, very purposefully mislead customers, coworkers, and probably darn near everyone else in their lives.

Lest you think I'm on some sort of morals high horse with a personal crusade to make the world a better, kinder place, let me clarify my purpose. I want to make the world of business a better, more efficient, more effective place. Lying is inefficient. Lying is ineffective. It doesn't work. It loses customers. And it is what will keep many companies from ever even approaching the status of being indispensable.

A Litany of Lies

It sometimes seems that the prevailing customer service philosophy of some companies is to lie. Often lies are told in the interest of telling the customer what they want to hear, or to spare them from the pain of an unpleasant reality. Indispensable companies understand that customers, like anyone else, can handle bad news. What they can't handle is either not knowing what's going on or being misled.

If you take me up on my "how many times are you lied to by companies?" survey challenge, I think you'll be shocked by how often it happens. You'll end up with a list that is a veritable litany of lies. It's almost as if being lied to has become normal. Business as usual. Just the way of the world. Let me once again say that I'm not taking a moral stand about lying. I'm taking a business stand about what works and what doesn't. Lying to customers is counterproductive.

The Truth Starts Internally

Lying is a leadership issue. Period. Either the culture in an organization encourages truth telling or not. Any indispensable company will tell you that the loyalty of their customers comes partly from being trustworthy. Trustworthiness is a cultural issue. Like any other aspect of organizational culture, it is more powerfully ingrained by example. Employees watch their managers and executives to see what the rules are. If leadership lies to them, then they have the stamp of approval to lie to each other and to customers.

A Standing Ovation for Bad News

A few years ago I was working with an airline on customer service issues. I was present at the airline's national sales meeting which was attended by every sales representative in the company, their managers, and all senior executives. The president of the airline was warmly received, as were the other executives as they delivered presentations about the general state of the company and plans for the future.

When one particular vice president was introduced, something extraordinary happened. He got a very loud extended standing ovation as he walked onstage. I didn't know what was going on, or why he was the recipient of such enthusiastic admiration from the employees. Even more interesting was that he was not a vice president of sales. He was an operations executive. Yet, these sales representatives were according him the kind of reception you normally see reserved for the beloved leader of your own department or division.

He began his presentation by laying out the reality of the market situation for the company and how that was going to impact the sales group. He asked the sales reps from a particular city office to identify themselves. They did so with wild applause and shouting. Things quickly got quiet when he looked at them and said, "I'm glad I'm not going to be working your territory this coming year." He then gave them the bad news, which involved some sales support issues that would affect them adversely and immediately.

He continued by telling others within the group the similar negative circumstances in which they would find themselves during the coming year. He didn't try to sugar coat one bit of the news. Nobody liked hearing it. This was followed up by a thoughtful and fairly detailed explanation of why decisions had been made and how they would hopefully have a positive impact on the company in the long run.

When he finished his presentation, he took questions from the audience and answered each one straight on, with no waffling, BS, or beating around the bush. At the conclusion of his part of the program, as he left the stage, once again the employees gave him an extended standing ovation. This time the ovation seemed respectful in nature, rather than celebratory.

After the general session, I was working with about a hundred of the participants on some competitive positioning issues. I felt that I had to ask about the way the entire group had treated this vice president. Why all of this obvious admiration? The answer was obvious and the one I knew I'd get. "He respects us enough to always tell us the truth. We trust him," one member of my group responded. Heads nodded in agreement throughout the room.

The philosophy of an indispensable company demands that you tell the truth to employees and customers. It builds trust. It commands loyalty. Here's the obvious but often overlooked fact: Good intentions aren't enough. Good intentions don't insure that all employees are giving customers the accurate information which creates trust. Truth has to be modeled, talked about, monitored, and rewarded.

We'll Be Departing on Schedule

I'd like to see the faces of airlines executives if they sat with me at gates in airports and heard their employees spout outrageously bold-faced lies at hundreds of customers at a time. Here's a classic example that all frequent fliers run into. The incoming plane that you'll be flying on hasn't arrived yet, it's five minutes until the time you're scheduled to push back from the gate, and all you want is an accurate arrival estimate to let the people meeting you at your destination know how late you'll be. When you ask the gate agent what the delay will be he looks at you with the straightest face God ever put on a human being and says, "We'll be departing on schedule." It's such a blatant lie that you can't even process it, much less respond to it. And those companies wonder why customers hate them so much. Ask anyone in that company, though, if they lie to customers, and they'll probably react with a shocked, "Never!"

Accuracy Is Indispensable

Will she call me back by the end of the day? Will I have this order by next week? Can you do this job within this particular budget? Can you assure me that I'll have the quantity I need?

You can answer "No" to every one of those questions, and I'll be your devoted customer for life. You will be indispensable to me. You will be my default first choice in business. Just give me accurate information, and tell me what you can do to help me solve my problem. Your customers can handle bad news. What they can't handle is not knowing what's going on.

Call Them on It

So what's a customer to do? I say if someone lies to you, call them on it, and, if possible, fire them on the spot with no second chance. Write the president of the company with precise information about the lie and document whenever possible. Tell her that the company lied, you're firing them, and you're going to tell everyone you know. What about second chances? Don't give them. Lousy companies have gotten by for too long on the good will of people giving second and third and fourth chances. Fire the offender, and take your business elsewhere.

The flip side of that equation is to reward and recognize those companies that tell you the truth. When Smith & Hawken told me in no uncertain terms the cushions I'd ordered would take up to six weeks to be delivered, I thanked them. I had begged and whined and tried everything I could to get them to say they'd deliver them sooner. No dice. These cushions take six weeks, and that's the end of that story. The result is that I remain a loyal Smith & Hawken customer because they gave me accurate, truthful information.

When American Airlines called me early in the morning a couple of weeks ago to let me know that my scheduled flight for that morning was delayed, I appreciated the bad news. It let me handle the situation. Most customers can work around almost any situation if they only know what's going on. Bad news can't become a habit, and if American Airlines flights are delayed too often, then they lose me, as would any other airline with which I do business.

I Didn't Show Up—I Was the Hero

In over 20 years of speaking for corporate events, I've not shown up on exactly two occasions. Ironically, both times the events were in Nashville, where I live. And both cancellations were caused by bad weather in the cities from which I was traveling. In each instance, my response was immediate and decisive.

I work through speakers bureaus, so in each case I called the bureau that had booked me for the event. We strategized about who we might call on to be a substitute speaker, were able to successfully line up a replacement, and let the client know every step of the way what was happening. It was handled so smoothly and with such accurate information to the client that in both instances I became a hero. It almost makes me want to not show up more often, but I don't get paid for not showing up.

The key was that each client commented afterward about how "taken care of" they felt through the entire process. They were given bad news, but it was accurate, and steps were taken to minimize the damage. People understand that things happen, and there's a natural appreciation for honesty and directness under difficult circumstances.

Do We Really Have to Be Reminded?

Does it seem as odd to you as it does to me that I'm devoting space in this book to a concept like telling the truth? Actually, I find it rather amazing. Do we really have to be reminded to be honest as a way of doing business? Yes. Some of us do. In interviewing people about what makes a company indispensable to them, one of the top factors was trust. It's one of those things that everyone knows but too many companies ignore.

Most would say that they don't lie, that estimates just don't work out right every now and then. But if it happens regularly, the customer calls it irritating, then incompetent, then dishonest. What some think of as the path of least resistance (to simply tell the customer what they think she wants to hear) the customer sees as the path to finding another place to do business.

9

Right Place— Right Time

Eat Here Now

My wife, Annette, and I were walking around the Upper East Side in New York City a few years ago. It was about 7:00 A.M., and I was starving. Here in the middle of the greatest city in the world all I wanted was something to eat, and we were coming up empty. There wasn't a restaurant to be found. As we searched block after block, my patience was wearing thin. It seemed like I was doomed to die of starvation right there on the street.

Like an oasis in the desert, I looked up and, hoping that it wasn't a hallucination, saw a sign hanging over the sidewalk. "Eat Here Now." That's all the sign said. Just "Eat Here Now." I'm assuming it was the actual name of the restaurant. If ever there was a succinct and effective product offering, this had to be it. I wanted to eat. I wanted it here. I wanted it now.

What this little New York restaurant had done for me was crack the code on what you have to do to make yourself indispensable to today's customers. You not only have to give them what they want, but give it to them how they want it, when they want it, and where they want it.

It's in the Right Place

The grocery store where my mom has shopped for years recently closed. I asked her where she was buying groceries now. She named one of the big chain grocery stores and said, "It's not that great a grocery store, but it's in the right place." In this case, you've got a store that really isn't even giving the customer what she wants, but it's where she wants it. Sometimes the "how" of the way we deal with the customer can even override the "what" in the transaction.

For me, though, the real lesson is to look at the concept of location in a really expanded sense of the word. Being in the right place at the right time with the right delivery of the right product is pretty much the universal formula for success in business. Today, however, the meaning of place, time, and delivery has changed to include factors that we hadn't even thought of just a few years ago.

It Depends

One of my clients is a very high-tech company that provides a lot of support for customers over the Internet. In a leadership conference with this client, the topic at hand was customer service support. I was asked whether or not today's customer still preferred to talk to a live person rather than go through an automated solution process over the Internet. I took a strong stand and said, without equivocation, "Yes. Today's customer does want to speak with a live person when solving problems or having questions answered." I immediately added, "Unless they don't."

To further muddy the waters, I threw in, "It depends." And it does depend. It depends on whether or not this is an old school kind of customer who places a premium on having immediate access to a live person to walk him through whatever it is he needs. Or this may be one of the new breed of customers who prefers that you please not complicate her life with the unpredictability of a live customer service representative, and she would greatly prefer you to just give her access to a purely web-driven "Frequently Asked Questions" process by which she can get whatever it is she wants. That customer's attitude is that she knows how to operate a computer so please just let her handle it without the messiness and inconvenience of having to deal with a person.

You also have to consider that one day I might want to speak with someone and the next day I just want to handle my problem by computer. It might depend on my mood or my particular need on that particular day. You have to give the customer what he wants, how he wants it, when he wants it, where he wants it. But the first step is figuring out the answer to those questions at any specific moment in time.

Open All Night

Remember the neon sign that you'd see in front of a classic greasy spoon diner? The one that flashed "Open All Night"? Sometimes it seems that there's a sign hanging in front of the whole world economy that says "Open All Night." When trying to become indispensable to a customer who is getting accustomed to obtaining anything he wants at any time, accessibility becomes a critical factor.

Commerce Bank is a financial services retailer with about 300 stores in New Jersey, Pennsylvania, New York, Delaware, and Connecticut. The Commerce Bank strategy is to physically take the bank to the marketplace in the form of an aggressive expansion plan. They are taking the "Open All Night" philosophy as a mantra, and are staking their claim to differentiation largely on being the most accessible financial services retailer in their region. They call their strategy a "have it your way" approach emphasizing the importance of providing customers with convenient, quality financial services, whenever, wherever, and in whatever way they want them.

While not yet literally open all night, Commerce Bank pioneered the concept of seven days a week branch banking with extended hours. Typical branch hours are 7:30 A.M. to 8:00 P.M. Monday through Friday, 7:30 A.M. to 6:00 P.M. on Saturdays, and 11:00 A.M. to 4:00 P.M. on Sundays. For years, Commerce Bank has also opened their branches at 6:00 A.M. on "Black Friday," the day after Thanksgiving, which is considered to be the busiest shopping day of the year. With many retailers opening earlier than usual on Black Friday, Commerce Bank aims to be open for business when its customers need it.

For an entire generation of consumers who have grown up having their wants and needs fulfilled on a 24/7 basis, this kind of accessibility is a no-brainer. Their view would be "Why isn't the bank open on Sunday? Why would it not be? Who came up with the lame idea that people wouldn't need to get a loan or open an account on Sunday?" Open on Sunday? Duh. Of course, the bank is open on Sunday. Just like the grocery store, the bookstore, and virtually any other kind of retail business you can imagine.

Finding the Balance

The balance that some businesses will have to strike, however, is that being open on Sunday or at night or at other times could conflict with either the strategic plan of the company or possibly with the personal preferences of the people within the organization. Some of my clients are among the most successful retailers in the marketplace, and they have limits on their availability, including, for some, not being open on Sunday.

This can be because, for their particular business, the numbers just don't work. The cost of extended hours outweighs the benefits in increased business or customer satisfaction. The trick is that you have to offer value in some form that counterbalances your competition's willingness to be available for business when you aren't.

In my own business, I have placed pretty strict limits on the amount of work I will take that involves weekend assignments. Being someone who speaks at a lot of corporate conventions, I'm knocked out of contention for a significant amount of that business. The balance is that I have a wife and daughter, and I actually like hanging out with them. I feel it's necessary to draw a line somewhere, and for me it happens to be weekends. In the long run, I feel that because it works for me personally, and contributes to my own sense of health and well-being, I can be more effective in my work and offer better value to my clients.

Nobody Does That in This Business

What Commerce Bank has done is take on the Sacred Cow of "banker's hours" and turn it on its head to create a clear competitive advantage. This takes courage. Very few companies are willing to walk into the face of conventional wisdom that says "Nobody does that in this business." Yet, what we will inevitably see is that the wildly radical innovation of extended banking hours will soon become the minimum expectation for entry into the market for retail financial services.

The next time you are in a hotel take a look in the closet. There you will see what was once a radical innovation in the lodging industry. You will see an iron and an ironing board. It wasn't that long ago that you had to call housekeeping to have an iron sent to your room. It never occurred to anyone in hotel management that it would make sense to just have an iron on hand for everyone right in their room. On the contrary, it would have been seen as a crazy idea.

Have You Lost Your Mind?

The next time someone in your company comes up with an idea that is obviously unrealistic and violates all of the written and unwritten rules for your business, take a few minutes to just say, "Well, why not?" and "Okay, what if?" At some point, that's what happened in a hotel manager's meeting, and it changed the rules for everyone in the business.

I like to imagine that at a regular weekly meeting of department heads in some hotel, the head of housekeeping raised what was probably seen as a staffing issue. With guests registering in droves during the late afternoon hours, housekeeping had the challenge of continuing to clean rooms while newly arriving guests were calling for irons to be sent to the rooms as they unpacked their wrinkled clothes. The obvious solution might have been to hire some part-time people to act as runners for the dozens of irons and ironing boards during that busy part of the day.

But somewhere, one day, at one of those meetings, some brave soul raised her hand and said, "Look. We've got twelve hundred rooms in the hotel. Why don't we just buy twelve hundred irons and ironing boards and put one in every room?" My guess is that this suggestion was most likely met with nothing less than full-blown jeers, hoots, and shouts of "Have you lost your mind?"

What were the objections? Someone probably pointed out that there was absolutely no budget for this kind of expenditure. Another naysayer surely observed that the guests would just steal the irons. And the entire room likely chimed in on a chorus of "Nobody does that in this business!" And today an iron and ironing board in your hotel room closet is about as minimum an expectation as you can have.

What Rules Are You Going to Break?

Once again, let's get to the teaching point for those who find it hard to connect the dots. In terms of your accessibility to your customers and your willingness and ability to give them what they want, how they want it, and where they want it, how willing are you to do what just isn't done in your business? Commerce Bank did it. Some hotel somewhere once upon a time did it with irons and ironing boards. What rules are you going to break that will become the next standard of performance in your business?

I do a lot of work in the car business. When everybody started making a good car, the auto industry realized that quality was no longer enough. In addition to making a good car, you had to win the battle of the parts counter and the service department. It became imperative to always be on the lookout for new ways to make yourself accessible to the customer.

Rules were broken. Convention was flaunted. Strategies such as making money doing oil changes were turned upside down and became free oil changes for life just to keep the customer coming back into the dealership. I saw an ad yesterday for a new car that came with a year's free oil changes. I laughed. A year? Really? Just a year? I didn't realize that anyone wasn't doing it for the life of the car these days.

What many auto manufacturers and dealers are taking a look at today is the concept of the completely mobile service department. This is a van and a service technician outfitted with the ability to perform routine maintenance and anything other than a major repair right in your driveway. It sounds like something that all dealers should be offering, and it may well be at some point. But right now it's still on the edge of the daring and unthinkable to most of the people in the business. Pretty soon somebody will break the rules and make the numbers work, and at that point it will become a minimum expectation in the marketplace.

Can You See Me?

One of the most valuable lessons I ever learned in business was at a McDonald's in Maryland many, many years ago. I was driving a rental car from Washington, DC, to Ocean City, Maryland, to do a speech for an AT&T leadership conference. In the middle of the afternoon, I was about halfway there and, because I hadn't had anything to eat that day, I was very hungry.

Seeing a McDonald's, I turned into the parking lot, which was completely empty because it was their down time, halfway between lunch and dinner hours. Purely by coincidence, a few cars and a couple of tractor-trailers turned in behind me. We all just descended on this McDonald's in the middle of the afternoon.

Being the first customer to enter the restaurant, I immediately took my place at the one open cash register. People began to form a line behind me, as we all waited for the immediate service that you normally get at McDonald's. This story is not, by the way, meant to be a slam in any way at McDonald's. I also want to stress that this happened many years ago, and I'm sure that no one who was working at that particular McDonald's then is working there now. What happened there could have happened, and does happen, anywhere. It's happened at my own restaurant, and I dare say that a version of it has happened at your company. It's a cautionary tale from which all of us can learn.

As we stood there waiting for service, the McDonald's employees behind the counter were busy as little bees, cleaning this and cooking that and putting things away. What's more, as they carried out their various tasks, each one of them would make occasional eye contact with us. It's not that they didn't know we were there. They were looking right at us! You've had this same experience in your life. We all have. It's one of those things that begin to feel surreal after a few minutes.

It got so bad that the guy standing in line behind me, who was one of the truck drivers and a rather large fellow, tapped me on the shoulder. When I turned around to see what he wanted, he said, while tapping his chest with his fingers, "Hey buddy, can you see me? I mean, I can see you. Why can't they see us?"

Good question. About that time, the woman in the drive-in window, whom I assume was the shift manager, turned and said, "Hey Michelle, get the counter." With a spring in her step and a smile on her face, Michelle approached the counter and asked, "May I take your order?" At this point, I felt the need to have a conversation with Michelle.

We've Got a Lot of Things to Do

I said, "Michelle, the folks and I have been talking among ourselves, and on behalf of the group, I have a question. How can this happen? How can you have eight customers standing in line at the cash register, all waiting for service, and nothing happen? You all saw us. In fact, you all looked right at us. And we can see you're busy. You might be doing something back there that you have to do in order to take care of us up here. But we didn't get that information, Michelle. We're getting no information. We're getting no Happy Meals. We're getting NOTHING here, Michelle!!!"

Michelle, with the sweetest face God ever put on a human being, said to me, in a voice weary with trying to be patient, "Sir, let me try to explain something to you. You see, we have a lot of things to do here besides just wait on customers." I couldn't even process it, much less respond to it. I was dumbfounded. Speechless. I stumbled into the parking lot with my sack of hamburgers and drove away in the afternoon, completely stumped as to how I should think about this.

The lesson, of course, has to do with the total experience that you create for customers, including, and often most important, the accessibility you present. One of the unforgivable sins in business is to have your customers saying or thinking, "Can you see me?" That means whether they're standing at the counter right in front of you, trying to find their way around your confusing web site, stuck in the endless maze of "for customer service press 3" in your phone system, or simply being ignored in any way, form, or fashion.

Never in the history of business has response time and availability played such important roles as competitive factors. The days of bragging because you return phone calls within 24 hours is over. Twenty-four hours? You're joking. Welcome to the twenty-first century. Tell me you return calls within one hour and you might have my attention.

"Whenever you want me, I'll be there." It's a line taken from an old Spinners song. It should be your mantra if you're looking to become indispensable. For a final example of the "How, Where, and When You Want It" school of indispensability, I offer MinuteClinic.

I Can't Go to the Doctor Today—I Have to Go to Target

You wake up with a cold. Sore throat, runny nose, aches, and pains promise to make your day miserable. Your loving spouse says, "Go to the doctor." But to make matters worse, you have to do back-to-school shopping for the kids today. You say, "I can't go to the doctor today. I have to go to Target."

MinuteClinic operates walk-in clinics for people with relatively minor health ailments, such as earaches, strep throat, bronchitis, flu, and seasonal allergies. Each clinic has at least two full-time nurse practitioners, and a physician is on call during all hours of operation.

MinuteClinic is setting up clinics in Target stores. Appointments are not necessary, and you can wear a beeper so that you can shop while you wait. With a pharmacy on-site at Target, it makes for one-stop health care.

Maybe I'm wrong, but this seems like a very cool idea. The lesson for your business should be smacking you around the head and shoulders full force. If you are having trouble getting your customers to come to you, then go to them. Figure it out. Stop waiting for the magic customer fairy to appear and sprinkle buyers on your company. And do not wait for the 10-step instruction sheet because it doesn't exist.

When done properly, business is among the most creative of endeavors. Indispensable companies don't follow the guidelines that made companies successful in 1997. That will only work if 1997 comes back. Indispensable companies make up new guidelines like opening clinics in Target stores.

Don't copy. Create. And while you're creating the next thing that will make your business indispensable, pay particular attention to being there for your customer at the right place, at the right time.

10

Case Study: The Pancake Pantry

Pancakes

On any given morning around eight o'clock the line begins to form. The place has already been busy for a couple of hours, but now people are lining up outside of the main room, into the entry lobby, out the door, down the side of the building, and around the corner. They will stand there, talking or staring or reading their newspapers, all just as happy and patient as most bluebirds.

If it's a weekend morning, then bring a bigger newspaper, because the line will stretch much farther down the block and your wait will be quite long indeed. Patience is a requirement if you want to get into this place. It's all a matter of supply and demand. What they have is something that no one else has.

They've got pancakes.

Art—Magic—Voodoo

The Pancake Pantry on Twenty-First Avenue South in Nashville, Tennessee, is, for anyone wanting to know how to achieve indispensable status with customers, the source of all knowledge. Bob Baldwin started something magical with The Pancake Pantry years ago, and David continues the show. Go inside, order some pancakes, watch, and learn. But you'd better leave your logical "just tell me how to do it," approach to business at home.

The Pancake Pantry is like virtually all businesses that have mastered the art of winning and keeping customers for life. The operative idea here is that what The Pancake Pantry does is, in fact, an art. Or maybe it's magic. Or voodoo. Becoming indispensable is always an art at least as much, if not more, than a science. There are countless companies in the graveyard of failed businesses that were perfect on paper. But for whatever reason, it simply didn't work.

The list makers and linear thinkers have a hard time with indispensable companies because they can't just take the template from them and lay it on top of their own business. Sorry. It can be really hard to come up against a concept like magic in business, but there it is. Indispensable companies are rarely perfect on paper, and they surely aren't everybody's cup of tea. It's only their customers who love them that, well, love them. Other customers may hate them and cannot for the life of them figure out what the attraction is. It can make an MBA graduate crazy.

It's the Mix

Cracking the code on how to win and keep customers for life is a matter of looking at the mix. It's not the individual pieces of the puzzle that make the whole picture. It's truly only when the pieces are put together in a particular way that you begin to get it. So what does The Pancake Pantry mix together that has made it a phenomenon?

You can start to see what a puzzle this idea of becoming indispensable is if you do a little Internet research on The Pancake Pantry. I'm not talking about their web site. If you go to PancakePantry.com, you'll get another restaurant. I'm sure it's probably a fine place. I just don't know anything about it. The Pancake Pantry in Nashville has no web site that I'm aware of. But Google them, and you'll get all sorts of articles and reviews to chew on. That's where the mystery of the mix comes in.

I Don't Get It

You may start by taking a look at articles about The Pancake Pantry in such publications as the *New York Times* and *Food & Wine* magazine. They use words like "legendary" and "don't miss." The local restaurant-reviewing web sites also chime in with glowing accounts of the nirvana for breakfast junkies that is The Pancake Pantry. Then it gets a bit confusing.

Read the actual customer reviews posted on the web sites and you'll see quite a range of opinions, from "It was worth the one hour wait in the below freezing weather to eat here," and "The pancakes are the best I've ever eaten," to "Prices not too bad and the service was okay," and "Service was just okay." But hold on. It gets better.

There's the guy who said, "I absolutely refuse to wait in line for something that I can get somewhere else for less money, while receiving better service. It's noisy, and there are lots of kids and a lot of pushy people. Go in the afternoon to avoid standing in line for a barely mediocre experience." A little farther down you'll see, "The service was great and the food even better. I will gladly wait in line for these pancakes." One customer laments that there is ". . . no pure maple syrup, Cool Whip instead of real whipped cream, margarine instead of butter." But then there is the woman who swoons over the ". . . homemade syrups and real butter."

At this point, you might be thinking "I don't get it."

It's a Mystery

In the movie *Shakespeare in Love,* when a producer of a live performance of a play is asked how the production can possibly come together given all the incredible confusion, missed deadlines, and general state of disaster that prevails, he says "I don't know. It's a mystery." So what can we learn for our own businesses from the mystery of the puzzle that is The Pancake Pantry? Let's look at some of the pieces of the puzzle, all the while thinking about how it applies to you.

Not Everyone Will Like Your Product

First, the product. I am a regular at The Pancake Pantry, and I think the food's pretty darn good. Not the best breakfast I've ever had in my entire life, but way better than most. Some people think the food's overrated. They probably don't come back. Some people think that your product is overrated. And they probably don't come back, either. No problem. There's not a company on the planet that can claim that everybody loves them and what they sell. There will always be people who don't like it.

So I think we have a lesson right there. Don't try to please everybody out there. You can't do it anyway, and if you try the result may be messing up the thing that your core market does love. For those of you above a certain age, remember New Coke? Figure out what works in a way that it attracts and keeps the number of customers you want and stick with it. Make improvements, change whatever you need to keep up with market demands, but don't dilute your formula. Remember that the goal is to become indispensable to enough of the market to make you happy, rich, famous, or whatever it is you want to be. You not only won't be indispensable to everyone, some people won't like you and never will. Live with it. That's okay.

Service with a Smile—Or Not

I love all the waitresses at The Pancake Pantry. I can really only talk about three of them, though, because of my seating preference for a booth. Sitting in a booth puts me in the area served by Joyce, Paula, or Betty. Each of them is great. Each of them is different. Each of them is a trip.

I almost always have breakfast with my buddy, Coke Sams. Coke is a film director and one of the great thinkers of our time. I say that because I almost always agree with him, so I think he's a smart guy. When we sit in one of Joyce's booths, we know that we'll be greeted by Joyce carrying two cups of coffee, saying "Hello, babies. How are my babies this morning? Coke, did you want coffee?" Coke sometimes does, sometimes doesn't. Our time with Joyce is always a love fest and sometimes a laugh riot.

When we get one of Paula's booths, it's a whole different story. Coke and I have known Paula for quite a while, and she usually comes to our booth and slides in beside one of us with not so much as a howdy and launches into a tale about her last grand adventure or big idea. Only after a few minutes of wacky banter and much laughing does she say, "So what do you want to eat?" Paula is a hoot. Paula is a delight. Paula is not Joyce.

Hang with me. There's a valuable lesson here for your computer business, gravel company, law firm, or department store.

When Betty is our waitress, we know that we will be met with a glowing smile and a long wait before she actually takes our order. I've actually told Betty that I was going to go grab a muffin somewhere to tide me over until she brought us our food. And I love breakfast with Betty because she makes the wait worth it. I feel like I'm at my aunt's house for breakfast when I'm with Betty, and she's the one that I show pictures of my daughter to every time I see her. Betty is wonderful. Betty is not Paula. Betty is not Joyce.

The business lesson for me is that the nature of the service that my company delivers can be somewhat different, or even wildly different, depending on which employee is doing the delivery. But the quality of the experience that is created must be consistent. The employee with whom my customer comes in contact must make that customer happy. Every time. That's how you become indispensable.

Your people don't have to be clones. They can't be and shouldn't be. But your people have to work together and with customers in such a way that the magic happens.

That's why company culture trumps anything else you do. Building a distinctive culture that works isn't just an important thing to do. It's the only thing to do. Your culture drives everything. At The Pancake Pantry they hire people who fit this eclectic mix.

I hear the cries out there: "But how? How do they do it? How do they find these people, and how do they know which ones to hire?" Well, it's like this. The culture of The Pancake Pantry is so overwhelmingly obvious and well known that they quite naturally attract the kind of people who not only fit, but who also stay. That automatically helps the process right there. If people don't know your company's unique style, how on earth are they supposed to know whether or not they want to work for you? Build your culture.

Look at any company with a large customer base that considers that company to be indispensable, and you will see that their employees are the kind of people who fit well with the culture. Southwest Airlines, Ritz-Carlton Hotels, Tractor Supply Company, Starbucks, Volvo, and every other distinctive company are staffed by distinctive people. All different kinds of people, to be sure, but all distinctive in a way that matches the company culture.

Pixie Dust

So you've got the pancakes and you've got the distinctive wait staff. What else do you need? You need whatever it is you do that completes the experience. You need something that makes you different and compelling. Call it *pixie dust*. Your particular kind of pixie dust will be different from The Pancake Pantry's, and theirs is different from mine. But make no mistake about it, there's pixie dust involved.

At The Pancake Pantry part of it has been that Nashville's country music industry has favored it as the breakfast destination of record. From the old days when you'd see Chet Atkins in the corner to the days of Garth Brooks and Lyle Lovett to today when you might find yourself sitting next to Vince Gill, the celebrity factor has been part of the pixie dust for The Pancake Pantry. It's just got a high "cool" factor rating.

Part of the indispensability factor is community. I don't mean that The Pancake Pantry has become indispensable because of its service to the community, although they've certainly done their share of that. I mean that The Pancake Pantry has created its own community of customers, who, because so many of them are customers for life, see each other there on a regular basis. It's a kind of networking glue that bonds together this very special and diverse collection of customers.

Don't think that the celebrity or community factors have nothing to do with you. If you're smart they have everything to do with you and how you make your business indispensable.

While The Pancake Pantry never actively had to seek out its celebrity customers, I know that part of my business strategy has always been to target the kind of marquee customers that I believe will attract others. A standard part of my marketing is to share with prospective clients a list of my existing clients. I know that the eyebrows go up when they see the other companies with whom we do business. They aren't celebrities in the show business sense of the word, but they are most definitely celebrity brands in the credibility sense.

The same thinking applies to community. I do whatever I can to bring my customers into contact with each other. Having my customers know and interact with each other does nothing but strengthen my position with them. (See more about this in Chapter 6, "Create Community.")

Throwing Paint on a Canvas

So in my business can I reproduce what The Pancake Pantry has done? Nope. Sorry. Not available. Neither can you reproduce what FedEx, Saks Fifth Avenue, nor BMW has done. You can learn the principles and apply them to your business. And you can work to find the pixie dust that will make all the pieces fit to reveal the puzzle. But the final frustrating lesson is that becoming indispensable is something that takes creativity, patience, and the willingness to find a groove that fits who you are, your strengths, and the wants and needs of your customers.

The longer I'm in business and the more I study successful companies, the more convinced I become that to succeed in business is a kind of artistic endeavor. Find an art gallery that has a work by American abstract expressionist painter Jackson Pollock. Listen to the occasional person say, "It's just a bunch of paint thrown on a canvas. I could do that." No, you can't.

Jackson Pollack threw paint on a canvas in a way that was magic. No art school can teach it. No one can reproduce it exactly. Business is no different. You have to throw the paint on the canvas in your own way, and the masterpieces are few and far between.

11

Big Picture
Outcome

What makes Ritz Carlton such a master of customer service and satisfaction? They understand big picture outcome in even the smallest ways. At the Key Biscayne Ritz-Carlton yesterday, I needed to find the ballroom where I'd be giving a speech. At the front desk, when I asked where my client's meeting was located, a Ritz Carlton employee named Andrea said that she'd be happy to show me to the room.

Andrea and the Walk to the Ballroom

On our walk through the hotel, Andrea and I struck up a conversation in which I told her that my room was fine, and that I was particularly impressed with something that room service had done to accommodate a special request I had made. I also told her that I was a consultant on competitive position, a writer of business books, and a fan of Ritz-Carlton Hotel's customer service consistency.

Andrea asked me if I knew the story behind their policy of escorting a guest to a destination in the hotel rather than just giving directions and pointing the way. I told her that other than the obvious courtesy of it, no, I didn't. Andrea told me that if they take the time to actually walk with the guest, it gives them the opportunity to have a conversation. In that conversation, the hotel employee can begin, as Andrea had done with me, to attain feedback about the guest's experience including what was particularly pleasing as well as anything that might have gone wrong or not been up to expectations.

"When we get that kind of information," Andrea said, "it then gives us the chance to both learn what works and to correct any problems that might exist. It enables us to create a deeper connection with hotel guests and create more value for them." Turning a simple walk into an information-gathering and problem-solving customer feedback session, my friends, is what's called looking at the big picture.

Creating a Big Picture Outcome

People don't buy products. People don't buy services. People buy outcomes. There's the old saying that you don't really want a drill, you want a hole. Indispensable companies understand that they are in the business of creating outcomes for their customers. More to the point, their employees understand it. It's a matter of having each person in the company be fully present in the sense of total engagement with what's really going on.

The Driver of big picture outcome is so vitally important that, even though it's included as a driver in almost every other story and example in this book, it's important enough to get its own chapter. Think about your own company and whether you are focused on creating successful transactions or the much more lucrative business of creating successful big picture outcomes.

This means that you have to go far beyond transaction, product, and service. You have to understand that each customer brings an entire set of wants and needs to the table and, to become indispensable, you have to address all of them. To create this kind of big picture awareness means that it's talked about all of the time, from training to meetings to, most importantly, the everyday interactions between all company employees. What's on everyone's lips and in everyone's hearts is this view from fifty thousand feet. A ground level perspective alone won't do it. You've simply got to see that big picture.

Beyond Job Performance

I have a maintenance contract with the company that sold us new heating and air conditioning units a couple of years ago. It's the standard six-month arrangement, in which a service technician does an inspection, cleans, adjusts, and generally keeps the systems up to speed and in good working order.

During one of these inspections, the service technician demonstrated a perfect example of being fully present and understanding the importance of seeing the big picture. It was what he did beyond the performance of the task that locked me into the company, and was the subtle stuff of competitive genius.

The Power of a Whisper

I have always had good experiences with this company, and James, the service tech, appeared to be carrying out his duties in the normally efficient, effective, and professional manner I had come to expect. As the time passed, I realized that our two-year-old girl was about due for her afternoon nap (I was on daddy duty that day and working in my home office). I told James that when he finished his work, I might be upstairs putting Jess to sleep and that he should just let himself out.

Jess went down for her nap quickly, and as I went back downstairs I spotted James coming into the house through the kitchen sliding door, having completed his outdoor inspection. What struck me as very subtle, and yet incredibly significant, was that James was taking great pains to close the door as quietly as possible, moving very slowly so as not to make a sound.

James looked up as I walked into the kitchen and whispered, "Is the baby asleep?"

I said that she was, and he proceeded to whisper his way through a brief report on the status of the heating and air conditioning units. Everything was in order, and as I thanked him for his work, James left by the front door, again taking great care to close the door without making a sound.

A Huge Deal

This is where I'm sure some readers are thinking, "Okay. So he whispered. How touching. How sweet. How touchy-feely of him. What's the big deal?" It's not a big deal. It's a HUGE deal. What James did with me gets to the essence of how companies become indispensable. James understood that he wasn't there to inspect heating and air conditioning units. James was there to take care of our home. It started, of course, with doing a great job with the inspection of the equipment. But beyond that, it involved that big picture view of what was really going on with his customer, and his response to my needs beyond that of the obvious transaction.

The real kicker to the story is that I couldn't for the life of me tell you the manufacturer of the heating and air conditioning equipment in our home. I don't have the first clue what brand it is. It works fine and I feel confident that I bought it at a competitive price. That's assumed. That's expected. It's not where the real competition takes place.

The battle for my loyalty as a customer was won, in this case, by a service technician named James who had a big picture awareness of his purpose, which was to take care of our home. For him, it was obvious that with a baby asleep in the house, you close doors quietly and you whisper.

There will be those who read this and think, "I don't get it." What a shame. Until you do, your chances of being anything other than a mediocre commodity player in the game of winning and keeping customers are slim indeed.

Simple and Extraordinary

What the lazy and the cynical will never understand is that while they look for rocket science approaches that will unlock the mystery of success in business, it's the incredibly simple, and equally incredibly demanding actions that create uncommon success in today's marketplace. While the many search high and low through every new business book for an explanation of the mystery of winning customers, the few who succeed know that they could read a thousand books and it still comes down to ordinary people doing extraordinary, yet simple, things every day, all day long.

The companies that become indispensable to their customers are the ones that grasp the subtlety and power of creating magic in relationships. Beyond big picture outcome, what my whispering HVAC technician did was engage, enchant, and enthrall his customer.

Creating a Mini-Friendship

I was at a convention in Dallas to deliver a speech on building your brand with the power of people. As so often happens when your antennae are out, as mine usually are since I'm always on the lookout for what works in business, the secrets of success will pop up right in front of you in the least likely of circumstances.

In the hotel where the convention was being held, there was a Starbucks. Don't roll your eyes. This isn't yet another in a seemingly never ending series of stories we read these days about the magic of Starbucks. This is a story about one young woman who understands the magic and power of the big picture, and how creating a relationship in a matter of seconds took the exchange from being just a transaction to becoming a kind of "mini-friendship."

It Changes Everything

Standing in a line of six or seven people, waiting to place my order, I couldn't help but notice that this Starbucks employee was making it a point to call every single customer by name. Sometimes she was able to easily see the name on the customer's "Hello—My Name Is" name tag that lots of us were wearing for the convention. If there was no name tag, she simply said "Hi, I'm Serena. What's your name?" when the patron approached the counter.

Serena did this with such obvious sincerity and quiet enthusiasm that it was simply compelling. There's no other word for it. Everyone's smile became a little brighter, and there was an aura of good mood around the coffee stand. She was able to have a short conversation with every customer, and it significantly changed the nature of what was taking place.

Serena was thoroughly professional and yet appropriately charming at the same time. Her use of each customer's name was the furthest thing from a cookie-cutter, memorized "technique" that she had learned in a training class. It was simply the only way she knew how to do business.

Being the inquisitive type that I am, I asked her about her use of customer's names. She said, "When I use a customer's name, especially in a brief conversation, it changes everything. For just a few moments, while they are buying coffee, we become friends. And that changes everything."

Slap Your Forehead

Aha! So, what Calloway is saying is that we should use the customer's name! Wow! Brilliant! What a wildly innovative insight! Let me slap my forehead in joyful surprise at this amazing advice!

The insight is that it's not amazing at all. The insight is that whether it's whispering because a baby's taking a nap, or calling someone by name because it "changes everything," the behavior is driven by a big picture view of what's going on. And what actually is amazing is that very few companies take a big picture view.

What's the Point?

In most companies, a new employee is told what the task is, what the job description is, and immediately begins training in how to do the work. They are never told what the point is. There's a focus almost exclusively on "what to do" and very little, if any, on "why we do it." And yet it's that big picture "why" that is the absolute key to achieving differentiation and becoming indispensable to the customer.

For James, the heating and air conditioning service technician, the big picture is to take care of the customer's home. The way he does that is by servicing a great product and wrapping that service in an experience that, in my case, included whispering. For Serena, the big picture is to give her customers the feeling of being among friends, even when away from home. The way she does that is by selling a great product and wrapping that sale in an experience that includes using my name and having a conversation.

Indispensable companies have great clarity around knowing what the point is, and how that knowledge drives big picture behavior. More importantly, it's part of their language. Mediocre companies talk about sales and transactions. Indispensable companies talk about the outcome that they want to create for customers.

Bring Jess to Me

When my daughter Jess was about two years old, I took her to a friend's birthday party. Little girls everywhere! They were running and playing and screaming with delight, until I heard one scream that was most definitely not with delight. Somehow Jess had been jostled around, fell to the floor, and landed on her elbow. From her cry, I knew that something was seriously wrong.

The party was just a couple of blocks from our home, so I drove by and picked up my wife, and off we headed to the emergency room. Now those of you who are parents, and even those who aren't, can imagine how very concerned and distraught we were. Our little girl has got something really seriously wrong with her arm, and I suspect it's a broken bone.

Even though it's Saturday afternoon and his office is closed, we call her pediatrician, Dr. Mallard, so that we can leave a message for him to pick up on Monday. Within about three minutes, our cell phone rings, and it's him. Dr. Mallard immediately asks what's going on, how is Jess, and where are we? We tell him our location, and he directs us to bring Jess first to him, at the YMCA where he is working out. "Bring Jess to me. I want to see her before she goes to the hospital."

We swing by the YMCA, and there is Dr. Mallard waiting in the parking lot. He gives Jess a gentle examination, says that he believes her arm is fractured right above the elbow, and sends us on our way to the emergency room with assurances about what to do and how to follow up with him.

He Got It

Dr. Mallard could have completely fulfilled his obligation to his patient by following up on our phone call on Monday. Or he certainly could have done more than was required by simply returning the call and directing us on to the emergency room. But Dr. Mallard understood that there was more going on than an injured little girl. There was a family that needed care. There was a scared and hurting child who would be comforted by a familiar face that she knows helps make her feel better when she's sick. There was a mom and dad who were scared and needing assurance about their daughter.

And there was a doctor who understood the big picture. He got it. He was helping create an outcome that went far beyond the symptoms of a broken arm. He was becoming indispensable.

They Didn't Get It

In contrast, at the hospital Jess got what I truly believe was the best technical medical care available. But she, and we, didn't get cared for in the Big Picture Outcome sense. They didn't get that taking X-rays properly and doing a good job of putting on the cast was just the beginning of what they should do.

The outcome they created was one of seemingly interminable waiting, not getting questions answered, feeling ignored and forgotten, and generally making a tense situation even worse. It wasn't personal. It was systematic. There was no one nurse or doctor who did a bad job. To the contrary, they all performed their duties admirably, except for the big picture duties.

I suspect that this hospital prides itself on medical expertise and excellence, and simply doesn't realize that it should be in the business of taking care of families and patients, instead of just solving the medical problem. It's a question of how it chooses to view its purpose. It gets back to knowing what the point is, as opposed to just what the task is.

This Is about You

Make no mistake, all of this is about you and your business. If, by some slim chance, you are unable to make the connection between your business and a whispering service technician, a conversational coffee clerk, and a doctor who says, "Bring Jess to me," then the problem is that YOU don't get it. And that's a serious competitive problem.

The principle of seeing the big picture applies equally to Internet companies, business-to-business vendors, one-person consulting firms, retail, manufacturing, service, and any other endeavor that you can name.

The first step, of course, is to figure out what outcome your customers want. And to ultimately decide what the point of your business really is. That's where the work comes in. It takes internal soul-searching and external customer research. In my own case, I had to get beyond defining my business by what was in reality just the delivery system for the actual product.

Don't Be the Coke Machine

I used to say that I was a business speaker and author. But as, my friend, Randy Pennington says, "That's like saying you're a Coke machine." What he means is that you shouldn't confuse the delivery system with the product. My product is ideas that help businesses build their brands and be more competitive. And in an even larger sense, I'm in the business of helping those businesses create certain outcomes. The big picture view includes making doing business a pleasure. It's all part of differentiating to get past the "me, too" commodity position of being seen as pretty much the same as my competitors.

The View from 50,000 Feet

Until every employee in a business understands the market power of a well-placed whisper, the value of changing everything through conversation, or the competitive advantage of getting to the heart of what the customer really needs, as in the case of Dr. Mallard saying "Bring Jess to me," then you will forever be at a disadvantage to the big picture companies that are indispensable.

I remember a time when a company would have one message, very strategic in nature, for top executives, a tactical message for managers, and a very task-oriented message for line employees. Thankfully, the days of only top executives having "the view from 50,000 feet" are coming rapidly to a close. Why on earth would any company not want every employee to have the same big picture view of the point of it all?

Of course, there are times when, depending on position and job function, people within the same organization will need to focus on different areas. But everyone should always be focused on one shared vision of who we are, why we're here, and the outcome that we want to create for our customers.

12

Twenty-Eight Indispensable Lessons

Right under Your Nose

Lessons on becoming indispensable are everywhere. They're in your garage. They're in your closet and refrigerator. They're right under your nose. It's terribly difficult, though, to get people to open their eyes and see what they should be doing with their own businesses by tapping the inspiration available all around them. This isn't about copying the other guy. It's about looking way beyond what your competitor is doing to spark some creativity from what people in other endeavors are doing. I always say that you could spend a day with virtually any type of company, from an auto dealer's showroom to the printing operation for a daily newspaper, and get inspiration for what you should and should not be doing in your own business.

Figure It Out!

I constantly beat the drum of creativity in business to my clients. In my 25 years of studying successful businesses, it has become glaringly obvious to me that the most effective leaders give their employees training, values, and parameters for action and then say, "You go figure it out." It's the old "give a man a fish and you feed him for a day versus teach a man to fish and you feed him for a lifetime" argument. Inspiration is everywhere. Whether you choose to be inspired or choose to whine about how there's really nothing you can do is up to you. The simple, and for some, painful truth is this: No one can tell you how to do it. What worked for one business cannot simply be overlaid onto another business with any assurance of success. The reason it can't is that pesky factor that always comes up: people. The ingredients used to bake a successful cake in company X are distinctly different from the ingredients you have in your company because people are all different. Any group of 10 people will be different in some ways from any other group of 10 people. Celebrate the differences, and use your creativity to figure out how to make them indispensable to the marketplace.

Lessons to Be Learned

In this chapter, I offer you 28 lessons on becoming Indispensable. The great challenge and opportunity is to figure out the lessons to be learned for your business and how to creatively discover your particular version of what can work for you. What will be even more productive is for you to make your own list of 28 or 50 or 100 businesses that you and your team can study for creative inspiration. Again, we're not talking about copying or taking someone else's fish. We're talking about learning to fish on our own.

Lesson 1: Have the Lowest Price

Want to be truly indispensable to a sizable market segment? Sell the same thing as everybody else and have the lowest price. I've got just two words for you. Or maybe it's more accurately one hyphenated word: Wal-Mart. In case Wal-Mart's lesson isn't clear, just look at their slogan: "Always low prices. Always." They throw in that extra "Always" just to be extra sure you get the message. Wal-Mart has its diehard fans as well as its critics and detractors. I'm not taking sides here. What I'm saying is that if you want to be indispensable to your customers, one way to do it is to have a price lower than your competitor on the same product. But there's a catch. Not many companies can make the numbers work. There's a science to consistently being the lowest priced player, and only a few companies have figured out how to make it work. You certainly won't find the answer here because playing the price game has never appealed to me. I've never pursued it, and I don't know how to do it. You could ask Wal-Mart directly how to do it, but my guess is that they're not giving away their secrets. But if razor-thin margins turn you on, more power to you. Knock yourself out.

Lesson 2: Compete against Lowest Price with Your Version of "More"

So how on earth can an ambitious big box retailer compete against "Always low prices?" One way is to take Target's approach, which is "Expect More. Pay Less." Aha! So the message is that we're competitive with prices, but there's more here than meets the price tag. Target has positioned itself as being the "upscale discount" retailer. Target is fun. Target is fashionable. Target is hip. Wait a minute. A discount retailer that claims to be hip? Check out Target's advertising over the past few years. It's generated a complete repositioning of Target beyond being just another discount retail big box to being a store with competitive prices that offers more through its unique product mix and more fashion-conscious marketing style.

Targets says they are committed to offering a fashion new-ness and excitement to their customers. That's the "expect more" part of the equation. Evidence that they are succeeding at this positioning of being chic, cool, and hip can be found in their inclusion in a special section of *Elle* magazine called "Dining by Design." It featured ads by some of the most respected design firms in the world, all in association with Taittinger Champagne. Some of the firms included in the section were such stylish companies as Robert Verdi, Calvin Klein Home, Coach, Ralph Lauren Home, Tiffany & Co., and, you guessed it, Target.

When you enter the marketplace as a low-cost provider, how can you go head to head with the 800-pound gorilla of low-cost providers? That's the challenge that Jet Blue faced when entering the same price market arena as Southwest. Their answer? Give the people what they want—low fares. Then give them more stuff that they want, like DirecTV and leather seats. You do what Target did. You take the value proposition and fatten it up. It's a numbers challenge, but when you make it work, the pay-off is market share. Some of the pertinent numbers for Target, by the way, would be their approximately $50 billion in annual sales and $1.8 billion (2003) in income.

If you've got a competitor who consistently charges less than you for comparable products, then here's your lesson. Figure out your version of the "more" that your customers can expect and give it to them in a way that totally separates you from the competition. It might cost you money, but it also might only take some creative positioning on your part. Don't play commodity. Take yourself beyond commodity in the customer's eyes. Create a new category and be the only one in it.

Lesson 3: Wow—Nobody Else Has This

The problem with trying to differentiate with product is that in today's world it takes about a nanosecond for your competition to come out with something even better. "Unique" is a fleeting state of being. But you can leverage product uniqueness into a market advantage, and there are lessons galore on how to do it. As Exhibit A, I offer you Wild Oats Natural Marketplace. Wild Oats is a chain of food stores whose, in their words, ". . . commitment to quality and our environment is unparalleled in the grocery business. We feature products that contribute to your health and well-being and we partner with vendors that meet our environmental and social standards." So right off the bat we know that Wild Oats has drawn a line in the sand and staked a claim for the environmentally conscious grocery shopper.

The challenge for Wild Oats is to clearly differentiate their grocery store in the eyes of this targeted shopper. How do they do it? Like this. I sometimes shop at Wild Oats, and I'm a fan of their take-out operation. They offer everything from roasted whole chickens to Greek pizza (yum) to a variety of side dishes and salads. The clerks always put my order in a clear plastic container like you'd see at any other take-out counter or deli.

One day I approached the counter and noticed a sign next to what appeared to me to be the usual clear plastic containers. The sign said: "Our new containers are made from CORN—an annually renewable resource. Please return cleaned containers to our store. We will deliver them to a local composting facility." Let me go back in case you missed it. The clear plastic containers aren't made of plastic anymore. They are made of corn. Corn. It's converted into dextrose, which is then converted into lactic acid, which is distilled into lactides, which are then bonded together into chains, made into pellets, melted down, and shaped into food containers. Think this might be a differentiator to the environmentally conscious grocery shopper? Duh.

Here's the catch. By the time you read this book, food containers made of corn may well be the standard in grocery stores everywhere. Probably not, but it's a sure bet that someone else is also using the same technology. So Wild Oats will have to come up with yet the next product innovation. Who knows? They may get their inspiration from learning a lesson from your company.

Lesson 4: Become a Way of Life

What started out as some souped-up cars racing for a few diehard fans on the beaches of Daytona, Florida, has become the mammoth marketing miracle known as NASCAR. For millions of Americans, NASCAR isn't just racing, it's a way of life. From the laundry detergent with NASCAR on the box used to wash their NASCAR logo clothes, to booking their travel on NASCAR.COM, to calling fellow NASCAR lifestyle buddies on their NASCAR NEXTEL Cup Series cell phones, NASCAR offers a masters degree in how you make a brand become an indispensable part of the lives of customers.

The absolute key to NASCAR's success is that they make their product personal. They know their customers, and they are masters at giving them what they want. From the old days of the spitting, tobacco-chewing stock car racer to the corporate entertainment monoliths that are today's race drivers (like Dale Earnhardt Jr. and Jeff Gordon), NASCAR is an organization that completely "gets it" in terms of how you get your hooks into a customer and reel them in to a position of complete and total loyalty.

It's all about the drivers. It's not about the "Number 2 car," it's about Rusty Wallace. If that Nextel cell phone is good enough for Tony Stewart's signature, race car colors, and car number to be on it, then it's good enough for NASCAR fans to move their phone business in a heartbeat. And that Michael Waltrip Jr. cap with the NAPA Auto Parts logo would make a swell gift for the wife on Valentine's Day. I'm not kidding. I'm talking about the "Ladies' Waltrip NAPA Auto Parts Cap" that you can purchase on the web site.

So where's the lesson for your business? Make it personal. It's not about your product. It's about the relationships you can create around the product. This isn't brain surgery. If a NASCAR fan loves Jeff Gordon because of the great interview he did with Katie Couric on *The Today Show,* then that's smart business. What are you doing to make your business personal to your customers? If they only know the product, and they don't know the people behind the product, you're missing a NASCAR-sized opportunity.

By the way, if you want to see how many ways an organization can create community with customers, check out NASCAR.com. It's amazing. Go there and be inspired.

Lesson 5: Be the Good Guys and Lesson 6: with a Great Product

If there was ever a company to admire, emulate, and from which to learn, for my money it would have to be Newman's Own. Newman's Own began when Paul Newman and his friend A. E. Hotchner made homemade salad dressing to present as Christmas gifts for friends and neighbors. Everyone wanted more. Everyone said that if they ever sold it, the dressing would be a huge success. Voila. They sold it and it was a huge success.

The first distinctive characteristics of Newman's Own is that only top-quality ingredients are used with nothing artificial and no preservatives. In the early days of the company, conventional wisdom was that you couldn't make the numbers work with this kind of quality product. Paul Newman once said, "There are three rules in business. Fortunately, I don't know any of them." His ignorance of what could and couldn't be done served him well, because he stuck to his quality guns and got the product made according to his high standards. The lesson for you and me is that people will pay for quality.   ●

The second distinctive characteristic of the company is that all after-tax profits go to charity. As a result of the sales of Newman's Own products, Paul Newman has donated well over $150 million since 1982. This qualifies the company as being one of the good guys. People like doing business with companies that do good things for the world. It's a powerful tie-breaker.

When you're shopping for salad dressing, popcorn, steak sauce, fruit juice, pasta sauce, or salsa, you've got lots of brands from which to choose. Many of them are great products. But throw in the fact that Newman's Own does good things for the world, and that becomes the tie-breaker that pushes the company into the indispensable category. The Newman's Own company slogan is "Shameless Exploitation In Pursuit Of The Common Good." People don't mind if a business makes money. People will enthusiastically support a business in making lots and lots of money if they know that the business is a good corporate citizen.

This isn't a book on being a do-gooder in the world. It's a book on becoming indispensable to your customers. Here's two ways that combine to become an extremely powerful force for differentiation: don't compromise on product quality; don't compromise on human values.

Lesson 7: Know Your Customers and Lesson 8: Change as They Change

In my work with clients I often ask audiences to talk about their favorite places to do business. In one such discussion a man said, "I like Home Depot. They sell me stuff I want." I'm not the smartest guy in the world but I have to say that this sounds like a pretty good formula for becoming indispensable. Sell your customers stuff they want.

There are lots of companies who work to do just that by creating a unique inventory mix based on knowing their target customer and exactly what that customer wants. In my last book, *Becoming a Category of One,* the case study was Tractor Supply Company, which credits much of its success to having a very unique product mix based on knowing what their targeted customer, the hobby farmer, wants.

When it comes to lessons on how to be indispensable through knowing what your customer wants, I find no better example than Oprah Winfrey. Yep. Oprah. If ever there was a master of selling stuff that the customer wants, it's got to be Oprah. Being a resident of Nashville, Tennessee, I remember seeing Oprah as a very young reporter for local television station WTVF. From Nashville, Oprah went to Chicago, and the rest is television, and cultural, history.

I believe that the key to Oprah's phenomenal success is that she understands her customers and she sells them stuff they want. Through her many endeavors, including *The Oprah Winfrey Show* (ranked Number 1 among talk shows) and *O,* The Oprah magazine (circulation 2.6 million in 2004), her goal is to transform people's lives by causing them to see themselves differently, thus bringing happiness and a sense of fulfillment into every home. In 2004, Oprah Winfrey was ranked by *Fortune* magazine as the sixth Most Powerful Woman in American Business.

There's a whole bundle of lessons to be found here. Like Paul Newman, Oprah has a great product and is most definitely one of the good guys. She supports countless charitable organizations and has been recognized for her wide-ranging humanitarian work. Her customers share her motivation to make a contribution to their world and Oprah gives them ways to do so.

In the incredibly fickle world of popular culture and media, talk shows and magazines come and go like the seasons. But Oprah has been a mainstay for years. You don't dominate in the media market without knowing what your customers want, and Oprah stays on top of her market. Oprah could be the most talented talk show host on the planet, but if her show dealt with topics that held no interest for her audience, she'd be history faster than a remote control can change channels.

For Oprah's season premier in 2004, she pulled off the ultimate daytime talk show coup of all time. This was the start of her 19th season, and Oprah wanted to catch the attention and imagination of the world. So what do you do when you've done virtually everything that can be done on daytime television for eighteen years? Do you give away more goodie bags to everyone in the studio audience? No. You give away a new Pontiac G6 to everyone in the studio audience. That's $7 million in cars that Pontiac gave to Oprah for Oprah to give to her audience. Oprah's theme for this television season was to "make wildest dreams come true." The members of her audience that day had been selected mostly from letters written by family members or friends who knew that they needed a car. The giveaway got incredible media coverage and was a worldwide sensation.

The lesson for your business and mine is to never assume that we know what our customer wants to buy today just because we knew it last year. We also have to be careful to avoid that trap of becoming stuck in something at which we're good. Like Oprah, I have to constantly reevaluate what has worked and be sure that I'm always moving forward, keeping my customers happy by matching my product offerings with what my customers want today. I've long admired the business sense of Oprah for staying just ahead of the interest curve of her audience. My hope is that I can manage to do the same for as long as she has.

Lesson 9: Be One Less Thing to Worry About

One of the oldest lessons in the business book is the power of consistency. A few years ago, I was brought in to speak to a customer convention for a client with whom I had worked for many years. This was about the fourth or fifth time I had served as a keynote speaker at this very large convention, the success of which was critically important to my client's business.

Shortly after I arrived at the convention hotel, I passed my client's CEO and his entourage as they walked down the hallway. He was deep in conversation with one of his people, and, even though we had made direct eye contact, he didn't say hello or acknowledge my presence in any way. Although I found it a bit strange, I went along my way and just chalked it up to his being preoccupied with the conversation.

"Hey, Calloway," his voice boomed from down the hall. I turned, and he was standing looking in my direction. "I didn't say anything to you because I'm in the middle of dealing with things I have to worry about. I don't have to worry about you. That's why I keep hiring you," he said. I took it as one of the highest compliments and best customer testimonials I've ever received.

A Federal Express manager once told me that the best thing about his job was that when he was working on a customer problem and had to turn it over to another department, he didn't give it another thought. He had complete confidence that it would be resolved. That's powerful. It's also the great lesson of Federal Express—when it absolutely, positively has to be there. One less thing to worry about.

When thinking about this particular lesson of being one less worry, it struck me that I can say that about very few companies. Just recently, I took some clothes, including a pair of pants that I wanted to have altered, to a neighborhood dry cleaner. After leaving the pants, I told my wife that my bet was that the pants would either not be done at all, or would be done incorrectly. When I picked up the order, sure enough, the pants had been cleaned and not altered at all. I left them there again with very clear instructions about the alteration I wanted. My bet is that when I go to pick them up they still won't be done correctly.

The real shocker is that I won't be surprised. It's a sad commentary on the state of consistency in business today.

On my desk, there is always a stack of FedEx shipping labels pertaining to packages I've recently shipped. I keep them because each label has the tracking number. Those tracking numbers are why I never give a second thought to a package once I've shipped with FedEx. It's not only my insurance, it's my assurance. I rest assured that everything will be delivered on time. It's truly one less thing to worry about.

I saw a yellow pages ad for a plumbing company that said, "We will show up exactly when we say we will. We will fix your problem exactly as we promise we will. And we will charge you exactly what you agree to in advance." It's sad, but true, that keeping promises, far from being the norm, has become a differentiator. My friend Larry Winget says that service is generally so bad overall that in a restaurant if a waiter shows up at all to take his order he feels like throwing a party.

Consistency of performance, dependability, being one less thing to worry about—these are all fast-track routes to becoming indispensable. If your way of staying in touch with customers is by constant phone calls to try and straighten out their complaints, you are what they are worried about, and they are eager to replace you. With all the stress in life today, being a nonworry is a huge competitive advantage.

Lesson 10: Make Life Easier

This could serve as a companion lesson to being one less thing to worry about. If you can make my life easier, I will give you my money. If you can make my life easier, I'll make you indispensable. The best lessons are almost always the simplest. Figure out what would make people's lives easier and do it for them. Then smile all the way to the bank.

My stock broker, Hall Haselton, makes my life easier by understanding what I'm trying to accomplish financially, drawing up the game plan to make it happen, and keeping me informed at the level I want, which is to not bombard me with information. He's the expert. I trust him. I let him do his job. In turn, he makes the financial part of my life easy by managing the relationship in the way I'm most comfortable.

Like lots of people, I am approached on a pretty regular basis by salespeople with various investment ideas and financial plans. On paper, a lot of them look good. The competitive obstacle they're all up against, though, is darned near insurmountable. For a lot of years now, Hall has made my life easier by conducting business on my terms.

On paper, somebody else might conceivably be offering me a better deal. But I don't live my life on paper. I live my life in person. And in person, Hall is indispensable.

Ditto for my accountant, James Weinberg. James explains taxes to me at a level that doesn't make my head hurt. He speaks in my language, not accountant language. I once told James to try and keep our tax-related conversations on about a fourth-grade level. James is brilliant with taxes. I'm not. He respects that and does it in a way that makes my life easier. He's indispensable.

Personal relationships can grease the rails of business so that the ease of the transaction overrides other considerations. Being easy to do business with and making the customer's life easier because of that can trump price and even product quality. It depends on the customer's priorities. In a marketplace that's hungry for personal attention, it's a critical error to ignore the power of the personal relationship in making customers' lives easier. Personal relationships aside, though, there's one Internet company that has earned my undying devotion because it makes my life much, much easier.

I recently traveled to southern California to visit two clients. I was flying into Orange County John Wayne Airport and staying at a hotel in Laguna Beach. I had reserved a rental car and would be driving myself to the hotel and to my appointments. Even though I travel to the Los Angeles area frequently and pretty much know my way around, I was going to need help in finding my way to my destinations. As I am a typical American male and therefore genetically unable to stop and ask for directions, I was facing a tough trip unless I did a little advance work to make my life easier.

On my list of web site "favorites" is MapQuest. I love MapQuest. For me, MapQuest.com is the poster company for businesses that make life easier. Here's why. I wanted to be able to drive from place to place with as little hassle as possible. I can go to MapQuest and type in the address of the car rental company. From there I get clear, step-by-step directions, with a map, to the hotel. Then I get directions from the hotel to my first appointment. But wait, I might want to go from the airport directly to the first appointment, and then to the hotel. So I get directions for that route, too. Finally, I get directions from the hotel to my next morning's appointment and from there back to the airport. I have every possibility covered. A combo of MapQuest both making my life easier and being one less thing to worry about.

The kicker? It's free. I don't pay a dime. MapQuest makes its money by the ads that are bought by companies, like hotels, car rental companies, restaurants, real estate companies (who knows? I might be there looking for a new place to live), and so on. The ads on MapQuest serve to make my life easier still, as they are for companies that cater to travelers' needs. It's a win–win–win situation all around.

If you position yourself in your market as being the choice that makes life easier, you stand a good chance of becoming indispensable. Look at your own list of indispensable companies, and I'll wager that a good number of them are there for that very reason.

Lesson 11: Know When It's Not Your Job

There's a great scene from a movie called *Joe versus the Volcano*. Joe's (Tom Hanks) boss in the movie is having a telephone conversation about an employee's ability to get a particular job done. The boss says, "I know he can *get* the job, but can he *do* the job? I know that. I know he can *get* the job. But I want to know if he can *do* the job." There's a big difference between being able to get the job and being able to do the job. Getting isn't the same as performing.

Among the worst professional decisions I've made are the few occasions when I took a job that wasn't right for me. Conversely, some of the best decisions have been to turn down jobs that weren't up my alley. The courage to say "no" to jobs and customers who aren't a good match for you, even when you need the business, can be one of your best assets in becoming indispensable.

A great asset that I've developed over the years is the trust that my clients and partners have in my willingness to say "no" when I'm not the best person for a job. I will happily and eagerly steer them in the direction of a competitor if I honestly believe that the other guy can do it better. If I'm not the best choice, then I don't want to be there. In fact, if I'm not the right choice, then it's the last place in the world that I want to be. Taking jobs you shouldn't take is a sure brand killer.

It's perfectly fine to want to stretch and challenge yourself with difficult assignments, but not at the expense of the customer, who might then suffer the consequences of less than the best quality work. If your strategy is to put all the business on the books that you possibly can, regardless of whether or not it's the right fit, then you are doomed to a false sense of short-term success to be followed by the reality of almost certain failure. Indispensable companies are quite comfortable with saying, "We could do that, but it's not really our area of expertise. Let us help you find someone who is better at that."

Lesson 12: Best Effort Every Time

Music is a big part of my life, and I have found a lot of lessons to be learned over the years by watching the careers of various artists. The world of rock music has a very long list of one hit wonders and a very short list of artists who have stood the test of time. When I think about those long-term success stories, I always look for the common thread. What is it that they all do that ensures customer loyalty and long-term success?

I've boiled it down to this: They give their best effort every time. That hit song from the 1960s that they've sung 10,000 times in concert will get their best effort when they go on stage to sing it the 10,001st time. Nothing lets me down more than to see an artist who just talks his or her way through a song as if it were an old joke and they're bored stiff. The same holds true for your business, whether you're a mortgage company or a sandwich shop. It might be the hundredth mortgage of the week for you, but for me it's the only mortgage in the world. Likewise on the sandwich. I will never forget the guy in a Subway shop who looked me in the eye before he took my order and said, "Sir, I'm going to make you the best sandwich in the world today. Watch this." The sandwich might not have been any better than any other I've had, but for some reason, it seemed like an award-winning work of art.

In the world of rock music, I can offer you no better example of being indispensable than the Rolling Stones. The first American tour by the Rolling Stones began in August 1964. I caught that tour on its Nashville, Tennessee, stop at the then newly built Municipal Auditorium. It was the first rock concert I had ever attended, and I was hooked. Through the years, the Rolling Stones continued to be, along with the Grateful Dead, U2, and Pink Floyd, one of the top grossing concert bands in history.

In terms of customer loyalty, consider this. I first saw the Rolling Stones on that 1964 tour, and I eagerly bought tickets for their 1997 Nashville appearance. Thirty-four years and about 20 Rolling Stones records, eight track tapes, cassette tapes, and CDs later, I was still a diehard fan, and remain so to this day. So what's the appeal?

For me, a big part of the appeal is that Mick Jagger, Keith Richards, Charlie Watts, and Ron Wood rock as hard on stage today as they did in 1964. When they do "Start Me Up" for the zillionth time, they don't sleepwalk through it. They burn from the first note and play it like it's the first time. I only hope that I give my customers the same fresh effort every time I go to work for them.

The same can be said for Bruce Springsteen. He was the first live act that my wife, Annette, saw in that same Municipal Auditorium. She says that she was riveted and has been a fan ever since. We have about 15 Bruce Springsteen CDs and saw him on his last concert swing through Nashville just a couple of years ago. It struck me that not only has this guy written more remarkable songs than any other writer of whom I'm aware, but that he put every ounce of energy and feeling into every note of every one of those songs in concert.

What I'm suggesting here is that if you or I approach our business with the same sense of pride and obligation to our customers as Springsteen and the Rolling Stones, our success will be virtually assured as long as we are delivering a quality product. You may have written countless loans at your bank, installed carpet in hundreds of homes, or designed more web sites than you even want to think about. But for me, your customer, re-member that it's the only loan, the only house, and the only web site in my universe. Give it your best effort every time, and you will become indispensable.

Short Subjects: Lessons One Bite at a Time

Lesson 13: Make it easy. Then make it easier again. The Bose Wave Music System is the simplest music system in the universe. It's the high-quality stereo for people who don't want a stereo; they just want the music. Bose made it easy to use with just a few buttons on the set itself. Then they made it easier. No buttons at all. Just a remote control.

Lesson 14: Remember what they're really buying. Harrah's has become one of the largest gaming companies in the world because CEO Gary Loveman keeps it simple. You don't go to Harrah's casinos for a five-star dinner or to hear the hottest pop star in concert. You go to gamble. Loveman has designed the business to cater to the person who loves gambling and will pay for it as a form of entertainment.

Lesson 15: Spend the money to find the next idea. Every company talks about innovation and is looking for the next great idea. Intel puts its money on the table. Intel Capital is one of the biggest high-tech venture capital companies in the world. It's all about looking for new ideas that might work with Intel's products. In your business, this might translate into just giving an employee with a wacky sounding idea the time and space to try it out. Lip service in the cause of in-novation is just conversation. Writing the checks for it is competitive.

Lesson 16: As a companion to Lesson 15, be willing to be wrong. Mistakes always give you information. Mark Twain once said, "I knew a man who grabbed a cat by the tail and learned 40 percent more about cats than the man who didn't." Thomas Edison once said, "To have a good idea, you have to have a LOT of ideas." I once said that I learned more from what I did wrong than I ever did from what I did right.

Lesson 17: Don't step over dollars to pick up nickels. I have competitors who think I'm an idiot because I'll buy a plane ticket to go see a potential client. These competitors do a much better job at saving money. They'll send a proposal packet instead. They won't even send it UPS or FedEX. Just regular mail. They tell me that they only spend $100 on sales efforts for every $1,000 I spend. They don't have $1,000. The reason they don't have $1,000 is because they lose their business to the guys and gals who get on the planes.

Lesson 18: The power of charisma. There are those who argue against charisma in business. They will make a case that the charismatic leader is, in fact, a long-term liability. They say that the charismatic leader develops a cult of personality and that the company will crash and burn immediately upon her leaving, so demoralized and aimless will be the employees. Charisma means having appeal. Having appeal means having influence. You don't have to be a dynamo of a pep rally speech maker to be an effective leader. But you do have to have influence. It comes down to this: Do I want to work for you? Do I want to make you proud of me? Do I feel good when you're in the room? That's charisma. And you can't convince me that it's not a big part of effective leadership.

Lesson 19: Generic marketing stinks. We live in an age in which *Reason* magazine sent a copy with a satellite photo of the subscriber's neighborhood on the cover. That's 40,000 subscribers—40,000 neighborhood photos. And in each photo, the subscriber's house was graphically circled. If you are sending out some junk mail, generic email, or paper newsletter when the rest of the world is marketing to one customer at a time, then you've got a problem. Wake up and smell the personalization. It's generally better to initiate one hundred incredibly personalized marketing efforts rather than one thousand "one-size-fits-all" versions.

Lesson 20: Pay for performance. Duh. I'm sorry to have to put this one in here. It's so excruciatingly obvious that it almost physically hurts. But too many people still don't get it. Payment for superior performance is one of the most powerful and fundamental motivators in the world. Krystal hamburger restaurants have a program called "Master Cashier." It's a special designation that is given to employees who demonstrate extra effort in being polite, friendly, and efficient. A Master Cashier gets a special shirt, special name tag, and, more significantly to some, make about $1 to $1.50 more than coworkers. In an industry known for rude employees and surly service, it makes sense to invest in those who can help differentiate your company from that negative image.

Lesson 21: Use the customer's name early and often. Does it get any more basic than this? Does it get any more powerful than this? Extraordinary companies put a lot of effort into using customers' names. Tractor Supply Company has a program that encourages employees to learn one more customer's name every week. See my book *Becoming a Category of One* (New York: Wiley, 2003) for more on this most remarkable company. The Hermitage Hotel in Nashville, Tennessee, credits its policy of calling customers by name as being a major factor in earning a five-diamond rating from AAA. That's five diamonds. That's the top, highly coveted, next to impossible to achieve rating. At the Hermitage Hotel, the bellhops wear earpieces and wireless microphones to alert the front desk that guests are arriving and to pass along the guest's name. Is this kind of effort worth it? Five Diamonds worth.

Lesson 22: Tell stories. Stories are infinitely more powerful than numbers. Want to know what has much more impact on employees than reading the company values at the quarterly meeting? Get Bob the delivery guy up onstage and tell the story of how he stopped his truck because there was a four year old boy wandering around a neighborhood. Tell how Bob called the police and stayed with the boy until help arrived and the parents could be found. Celebrate Bob with an award and a check and give him a standing ovation from everyone in the room. It's what FedEx Freight did at a meeting I attended, and it did more to drive home the company's values than any PowerPoint presentation could ever do. It's the same with customers. Tell them a story by which they can experience your business. It's a tough sell with numbers alone.

Lesson 23: Change the way people buy it or use it. It's not the gas that counts anymore. Most people think all gasoline is the same. Now it's about how you buy the gas. It's the pump that takes your credit card. Or the pump that lets you use your speed pass card which you don't even have to insert. It's not the Dutch Boy Paint anymore. It's the easy-to-use paint jug that it comes in. It's not the Subway sandwich that tastes good. It's the Subway sandwich that can help me be healthy and fit. Think about how your product is delivered and used. Your differentiating innovation may be there.

Lesson 24: The best location is to be everywhere. You can literally be almost everywhere, like Walgreen Drug Stores. If there's not one on every corner in your town, there may be by the time this book comes out. Or you can simply make contact with the customer on a regular basis. I did it for years with postcard mailings. Today, the Internet gives you the same opportunity. You just have to be very careful that you don't alienate anyone by being there when they don't want you. There is no Saks Fifth Avenue store in my city, but Saks Fifth Avenue sends me regular e-mail updates on what's going on. I like it. They're cool, and I want to know what their take is on merchandising and fashion in the marketplace. Plus, I like their clothes. So as both a marketing consultant and as one of their customers, I like to hear from Saks Fifth Avenue. *BUILDING PASSIONATE, THINKING, HIGH PERFORMANCE ORGANIZATIONS*

Lesson 25: Six words or less. Sum up what you do for customers in six words or less. It's powerful. More powerful than any three-paragraph, consultant-driven mission statement. I once worked with a health care company specializing in emergency wound treatment. In a manager's meeting, I kept pressing one woman to boil down the mission statement into a gut level idea. I pushed her and pushed her until she finally blurted out, "We help people when they're hurt! OKAY?" Bingo. We help people when they're hurt. In the discussion that followed, it turns out that this six-word statement of purpose resonated with and inspired the group much more than the mission statement ever did. Boil it down. Make it personal. Six words or less. What's the point of what you do? What GOOD do you do in the world? There's power there. Find it.

Lesson 26: Let your coworkers and employees surprise you. General George Patton Jr. once said, "Never tell people how to do things. Tell them what to do, and they will surprise you with their ingenuity."

Lesson 27: Take something out. 7-Up takes out the color and the caffeine. Hanes is taking the tags out of T-shirts.

Many merchants have dropped the need to sign your credit card slip if the purchase is under a certain amount. Look at your product or service, and figure out how you can improve it by taking something out.

Lesson 28: The market decides. If your competition is winning the battle for customers, then it means that they've got what the customer wants, and you don't. Being in a state of denial will only hurt you more. You don't decide who wins. Your customer does. Listen to him.

13

Case Study:
Pinnacle
Financial Partners

If You Could Make It Up

I've always maintained that the coolest thing about business is that it is a wildly creative endeavor, or can be, if you do it right. Every day we get to go back out there into the marketplace and just make it up. We can do what we do in any way we choose, and the market will tell us whether or not it worked.

So if you could make up any business you wanted, from scratch, and build it from the ground up in any way you want, what would it look like? Terry Turner did just that. This is the story of what it looked like.

Beyond a Pound of Nails

I do a lot of work in the financial services industry, and it's pretty much a commodity business the way most of the players do it. They have products that look the same, have offices that look the same, have ads that look the same ("We're part of your community!"), and have people who act the same. The biggest challenge for banks is to get beyond commodity and find meaningful, sustainable, and hard-to-replicate ways to differentiate from the competition. In lieu of differentiating, they end up being driven almost totally by price. To most bank customers, it's like buying a pound of nails. A pound of nails is a pound of nails no matter where you buy it, and the only difference is price. Terry Turner decided to start a bank, and to transcend the "pound of nails" commodity label in everything that the bank would do.

There's Another Way to Play This Game

Terry Turner had been with a big regional bank for 17 years, and had quite a successful run. But as mergers and acquisitions swallowed up the regional banks, Terry saw an opportunity to do things differently. He felt that too often client services deteriorated at the expense of a bank's inward focus to consolidate. He did research, considered the possibilities, and incorporated Pinnacle Financial Partners in February 2000. Terry decided to play the banking game according to a new set of rules.

The basic strategy was to target small businesses and their owners, which was just about the whole business market in Nashville, Tennessee, home of Pinnacle. The other target was affluent households with $250,000 or more in investable assets. This extremely attractive market was most definitely in the crosshairs of the competition, so Pinnacle had to create distinct and strong differentiators if it was to succeed.

The foundation of the strategy was, and is, people. Terry hired experienced professionals with large client followings away from other area banks, believing that many, if not most, of their clients would move with them. Associates at Pinnacle have an average of 24 years' experience as bankers or brokers in the Nashville market. Most of them hold securities licenses, financial planning certificates, or insurance licenses. Their financial skills and wisdom run deep. They know what they're doing. As Terry puts it, "Pinnacle simply will not entrust its valuable clients to trainees." The strategy worked. Hire the best people you can, and it will pay off.

The Pinnacle approach is a very people centric one. It takes an unwavering focus and commitment of leadership to make it work. Is it worth the effort? One hundred percent of the respondents to Pinnacle's client service survey say Pinnacle is recognizably better than its competitors. Additionally, Pinnacle has been recognized by the *Nashville Business Journal* as the "Best Place to Work in Nashville" among midsized companies.

The Differences

I asked Terry Turner to talk about what makes Pinnacle different.

Calloway: How important is it to Pinnacle's success that you have such a clearly defined target market?

Turner: Pinnacle's target clients include affluent consumers and owner-managed businesses. To give you a little more insight into how we define those targets, by *owner-managed* businesses, we mean businesses other than public companies. Nashville is predominantly a small business market. There are roughly 30,000 businesses located in the Nashville area. Of those, 29,700 businesses have sales less than $25 million. So Pinnacle focuses on and has the capacity to bank 99 percent of the businesses in Nashville. Regarding affluent consumers, we define affluent consumers as those households with investable personal assets greater than $250,000. At over 40 thousand households, this is a fairly large segment of the total MSA households.

Calloway: Okay, so you've got this extremely attractive target market that by definition is exactly who your competition is after. Most people see banks as being pretty much the same. How to you differentiate?

Turner: Pinnacle offers distinctive service and effective advice that's hard to obtain from big banks. The distinctive service and effective advice take a lot of different forms.

We have friendly professionals who know your name and financial situation, and these individuals will be there the next time you come in. Pinnacle's annual associate retention rate is 96 percent versus only 65 percent to 75 percent at the large regional banks in our market.

Availability and knowledge of decision makers is another clear advantage. Most clients know or have access to Pinnacle's executive management. Most clients find it distinctive to visit directly with the folks who have the capacity to commit the legal lending limit of the bank, as opposed to never speaking with important decision makers in another city, as is the case with a lot of the bigger banks.

Calloway: You're up against big banks that have locations everywhere. You've got a handful of offices. With convenience being a top-of-mind feature that bank customers want, how can you effectively compete?

Turner: We've got a courier deposit pick-up system, so that many clients never have to even come to the bank to make a deposit. This has put Pinnacle in the position of saying that we are more convenient than your current bank, even if you bank at a branch next door.

Calloway: In terms of what has come to be expected, like ATMs and online banking, what do you do that the other banks either can't or aren't willing to do?

Turner: Our customers get unlimited usage of virtually any ATM in the world with no surcharge fee, as opposed to being limited to the machines of one's own bank to avoid surcharges.

We've got a state-of-the-art online banking system that includes things like front and back images of checks that have paid against the account at anytime during the life of the account. Many large regional banks provide no check images online. The few that do are generally limited to the front of the check only. And all that I am familiar with limit information to the current month or year. None other than us offer unlimited access for the life of the account.

People—People—People

For all of the techno-coolness of showing images of checks online, it's not technology that Pinnacle is counting on to keep them on a very fast track of growth. It's the people. Repeat after me: "It's the people." The cornerstone of Pinnacle's success is its unique approach to managing and leveraging the asset of people. For those of you who find that the "people factor" in business is the most difficult to get a handle on, read and learn from what Pinnacle has done.

Pinnacle's mission, values, and vision were created by the firm's initial associates before it even opened for business. And, much like employees for Tractor Supply Company, the primary case study in my previous book *Becoming a Category of One,* new associates go through a three-day training and orientation process primarily done by the CEO.

Many companies struggle with the issue of employee commitment, but Pinnacle is totally on top of the critically important Driver of create and sustain momentum, and it starts from an associate's first day on the job. The key is that, early on, you focus on the point of the job, and not just the task. This also ties into the Driver of big picture outcome from an internal perspective. Employees who see how they fit into the company's vision and mission in a big picture way are more likely to be motivated and committed.

Another unique aspect of Pinnacle's hiring is that members of the Leadership Team hire the associates that they need to achieve their plan. In other words, they are not reliant on a Human Resources Department. Pinnacle does not take applications. They generally do not hire people who send them a resume. Their view is that those people are usually unhappy or unsuccessful where they are and, consequently, don't really fit the Pinnacle hiring profile. For critical hires, the CEO typically takes the lead in recruitment.

Pinnacle begins to marry the Drivers of create and sustain momentum and big picture outcome during the recruitment process. Terry Turner says that they spend a lot of time ensuring that potential associates understand key differences between Pinnacle and other large regional banks from which the potential associates are likely coming. Critical distinctions include that there is a philosophical fit and that the recruit actually "buys-in" to some basic tenets, including the fact that Pinnacle is a values-driven organization. The recruit will understand that Pinnacle cares deeply about and will measure individual performance, but that they care more about team performance. Potential associates will know that their monetary incentives are a function of how well the firm does, not how well the individual does.

Once a new associate comes on board with Pinnacle, an ongoing and never ending process of engagement works to reinforce all Five Drivers:

1. Create and sustain momentum.
2. Develop habitual dependability.
3. Continuous connection.
4. Big picture outcome.
5. Engage, enchant, and enthrall.

Pinnacle's ongoing associate engagement process includes:

- Three-day orientation conducted by the CEO that includes exercises to enable associates to buy in to the firm's mission, vision, values, and so on as well as physical team-building exercises at the YMCA.

- Monthly meetings with all associates to review the firm's performance against its targets and BHAGs (Big Hairy Audacious Goals).
- Environment of independence and autonomy that is easily facilitated by hiring only experienced, successful associates.
- Quarterly "listening sessions" by the CEO to gather feedback and solicit suggestions.
- Book Clubs that are available to all associates conducted by the CEO at his home. Books that hold some applicability to Pinnacle are discussed and then a meal is served. Approximately 75 percent of associates volunteer to participate.
- Annual Work Environment Survey in which 100 percent of associates provide feedback on the work environment. All unedited results are made available to associates along with Leadership Team responses.
- Frequent community projects such as volunteering for Special Olympics, building an affordable home for an individual with Down's syndrome, and so on.
- Regularly scheduled family events such as spring cocktail party at the CEO's house, family summer picnic at the riverfront home of a member of the Leadership Team, Christmas party at the Chairman's house, and so on.
- Frequent celebrations for major milestones and anniversaries, and so on.
- Annual cash incentives, based on the firm's performance, for all associates.
- Annual stock option grant for all associates.

Recognition and rewarding of associates' achievements also plays a critically important role in employee satisfaction and retention. Recognition and reward activities include:

- Simple thank you notes, e-mails, gift certificates, recognition in front of peers, and so on.
- At each monthly "all associate" meeting, several associates are recognized in front of the group for outstanding performance or living out the Pinnacle values in a demonstrable way.
- The basic annual cash incentive system in which all associates participate is primarily based on the firm's performance against profitability targets. However, it is not a fixed amount. The farther the firm exceeds the profitability target, the higher the incentive payout. Additionally, Leadership Team members have the discretion to award up to 5 percent of someone's base pay for extraordinary individual performance.

A sampling of comments from Pinnacle's Annual Work Environment Survey testifies to the level of employee satisfaction. Having seen all of the comments that employees submitted, let me assure you that there was the occasional observation about something with which an associate was less than satisfied. The comments are unedited and are available to all associates. But the vast majority of comments were along the lines of the following:

- So far my employment experience has been fantastic!
- Moving to Pinnacle was the best decision that I have made regarding my career.
- Pinnacle is a great place to work!
- Continues to be a good place to work. Staffing continues to improve. Needs to remain a focus as profits allow.
- I like to be on a winning team. I hope we keep the client first as we grow larger. The people are top notch. Please continue to only hire the best.
- Pinnacle is an awesome place to work. . . . It is wonderful to work with and be surrounded by people who have the

same work ethic and who honestly put customers first. . . . Pinnacle also cares about employees that in turn creates a much healthier work environment.

- I want to make sure we always keep a team focus in our Small Business area. I think that with the new hires we have planned, we keep the values in mind. Yes, we have to have a book of business but integrity, responsibility, and morals go a long way.

Bottom Line

So, if you could make up a business any way you wanted, and you did it like Terry Turner and his team at Pinnacle, what would it look like beyond the warm, fuzzy stories? What's the bottom line? So far, it's been an amazing ride.

Pinnacle's growth has been unusual as evidenced by the fact that of the 181 commercial banks chartered in the United States in the year 2000, Pinnacle is the largest and fastest growing. Pinnacle has become the largest locally owned bank in Nashville.

The company's stock performance has been consistently exceptional. Here are a few recent comments of financial services industry analysts about Pinnacle's market position and future prospects:

- "Balance sheet growth was nothing short of robust, in our opinion, as Pinnacle's client-oriented business model continues to dominate Nashville. There is no doubt in our minds that Pinnacle's management team is building an extremely valuable core community banking franchise."
- "PNFP is a fast-growing, urban community bank in the early stages of its growth cycle that is building one of the premier small-cap banking stories in the southeast. Given management's extensive market knowledge, deep customer contact base, and scarcity of local community-based bank holding companies (BHCs); we believe PNFP should

continue to deliver above-average growth rates over the foreseeable future."

- "PNFP continues to gain market share by investing in human capital and remaining sharply focused on serving its targeted customer base."

It comes down to this: In what is generally considered by the market to be a commodity business, Pinnacle has distinguished itself with the execution of practices and strategies that are available to any business anywhere. We don't get hurt by what we don't know. We get hurt by what we know but don't do. Pinnacle does what works.

14

Repeatable Process

Is It in the Genes?

I'm on American Airlines flight 1088 from Nashville to New York. The flight attendant has been doing a great job—that perfect balance of thoroughly professional and warmly personable. So far—so good, but nothing really indispensable is going on. It's just a pleasant flight, and all is well.

The move toward indispensable came when the attendant approached me and said that she had seen from her passenger list that I was a two million mile flier with American Airlines. She said that, in this time of great stress and uncertainty for all airlines employees, she greatly appreciated my continued patronage. She then offered her hand and thanked me for "providing my paycheck." It's not a huge deal, but it made an impression. She went out of her way to thank me. Very few people do. I noticed. Indispensable companies become so through continuously making just that kind of impression.

I'm a very frequent flyer on a number of airlines, so I can roll out the travel customer service stories almost without end. What intrigues me about this particular incident, though, is my curiosity about exactly what prompted this flight attendant's behavior. It's probably not the direct result of a formal training program, although it certainly could be.

Maybe it's just genetics. Maybe she was born with some special relationship-building gene that drives her actions. Or maybe her parents raised her that way, or modeled such behavior throughout her life. If so, then the goal of a business should be to figure out how to identify and hire such inherently talented people. Personnel consultants exist who have such programs, and many companies take full advantage of their services.

Removing the Element of Chance

But what if we could stack the odds in our favor in terms of making those kinds of favorable impressions take place? How do we ensure that positive employee behavior with customers happens almost every time? What can we do to make becoming indispensable the rule, rather than the exception?

You must remove, or at least minimize, the element of chance. This is the single greatest failing of many potentially indispensable companies. There's no pattern of repeatable behaviors that gets beyond the entry-level market expectations of having competitive product, price, and service. They're stuck at the commodity level and, while rejoicing over and celebrating their occasional "superstar" moments of customer service, there is simply no predictable pattern of positive behavior.

You Don't Want Superstars

The problem with superstar behavior is that it is, by definition, above and beyond. What you want is a whole different standard of behavior that makes extraordinary interactions with customers to be seen as the rule, not the exception. Then you can celebrate everyone's actions and the fact that you've become indispensable as well. What is considered over and beyond superstar stuff at your competitor's company will just be considered business as usual at your place. That's differentiation. That's indispensable.

The goal is regular people doing extraordinary things with customers every single day all day long. Don't think that I'm being wildly unrealistic. Look at the literal of the word extraordinary. It means uncommon, exceptional, remarkable, wonderful, or great. And we're talking about extraordinary as compared to your competition, not as compared to the other people on your team. Remember, the goal is to make the extraordinary become normal within your indispensable organization.

You Want Process

Go back to my flight attendant for a moment. It could very well be that she has implemented her own process of checking the passenger list for high mileage customers and thanking each one personally for his or her business. So it's not a hit or miss thing with her. It happens every time. It's like bringing out the pretzels or taking people's coats to hang in first class. It's a repeatable process. It's every time.

Staying on the airline theme, think of those times when you've been pleasantly surprised by a pilot who stood in the doorway as all the passengers filed out. He or she was taking the time to greet each one of us and thank us for our business. And you get the very distinct impression that this is something that happens with this pilot on every single flight.

Kind of makes you go "Hmmm. I wonder why every pilot doesn't do that." It's such a simple thing, yet makes a great impression and is just one of the many tiny great impressions that turn into becoming indispensable. That pilot has created a process that drives him to re-create positive action every time with every customer.

So What's the Big Mystery?

Here's where most companies lose me completely. People rant, rave, gnash their teeth, and pull out their hair because nobody can give them a way to implement extraordinary performance. They growl at smarty-guys like me who write books and do case studies and offer what seems to me to be my own unassailable logic, and yet we "tend to come up short on the how-to part of it."

Well, duh. Let's put on our thinking caps and see if we can wrestle this one to the ground before it does too much further damage. The question on the floor is: How can we drive positive behavior on a consistent basis?

Now this is just me talking here. Just thinking out loud. But what if, just what if, we made the desired behavior a requirement along the lines of turning on the lights in the morning, making the coffee, and unlocking the front door at 9:00 to let the customers in. I mean really, if we can unlock the front door every morning at the same time, why can't we just as easily do all sorts of really cool things like learn customers' names, thank them for their business, never leave anyone on hold for more than 15 seconds, return each and every phone call within one hour, or whatever else you wish you did but just can't figure out how to make happen!

What Gets Measured—And Other Things Obvious to All

We've all heard the old business rule that what gets measured gets done. True enough. And what gets talked about all the time becomes important along with what gets rewarded and recognized. So start measuring, talking, rewarding, and recognizing.

I work with a lot of financial services companies. Banks, in particular, are pretty much aware of customer satisfaction studies that prove the tremendous impact of the initial greeting of customers in relation to their satisfaction and, more importantly, loyalty. Most banks talk a great game of making that first impression a good one and always greeting each customer like the valued asset that he or she is. At meetings and pep rallies, there is much hue and cry about this all-important greet-them-at-the-door factor. And that's often where it ends.

Back to work they go, and no one creates a repeatable process, or the responsibility, or the authority to set up a means by which greeting of customers in a positive and consistent manner becomes a reality. There's no measurement of it and not even any further discussion of it once the daily grind goes back into motion. If you're not measuring it, then it's a pretty good bet that nobody's doing it.

Well, okay smarty. How would YOU make it happen?

I'd put the officer closest to the front door in charge of it with a back-up if she's busy, and I'd make the branch manager the overall hall monitor as a fail-safe system in case both of them are busy. Beyond that, I'd have the tellers keep a roving eye, occasionally checking to see if they need to pitch in with a friendly wave or hello, and I'd be sure it was talked about every day on a regular basis. I'd catch people doing a great job of it, then reward them. I'd be on the lookout for when it wasn't being done and take corrective measures when necessary. After making this a priority for six months, it would become as natural as breathing.

How Does Anything Happen Consistently?

If it's important to know customers' names, then I'd do what Tractor Supply Company does and have a "one new name a week" policy. Each employee with customer contact memorizes one new customer's name a week. I'd quiz them on it, reward success, and correct failure.

If it's important to know everything possible about our commercial customers' businesses I'd build a meeting a week around the reporting of research results and what opportunities for new business can be created from it.

If it's important to solve customer problems as soon as possible I'd give that authority, not just the responsibility, to every employee and turn them loose to do the right thing. And I'd talk to them about it all the time. We'd celebrate the victories, and we'd discuss and reexamine any missteps. But they'd never be punished. You don't give people the authority, then pull the rug out from under them when they use it. It's the oldest leadership mistake in the book.

Hoping for a Different Person

In the absence of a repeatable process to ensure consistency of performance, the strength of your company becomes a game of chance. Top-flight performance consultant Lew Carbone says that you can't NOT create a customer experience. It's just a matter of whether the experiences you create are by chance or by design.

Not too long ago, I called an insurance company's customer service line with a question about whether or not we could do something a particular way under our existing policy. A very nice person pulled up our policy and politely but firmly informed me that, as our policy was currently written, the answer was no.

I thanked her, hung up the phone, and immediately dialed the customer service number again. You know exactly what I was doing. I was hoping to get a different person, which I did. I asked customer service representative number two the same question, and she happily informed me that I could most certainly do what I wanted to do, and that all it would take was a simple notation by her in our record.

You might think that this is a customer service story with a happy ending. Quite the contrary. This is a story about a brand in trouble. If my satisfaction depends on who I happen to get on the phone, or across the desk, or behind the counter, then there's serious trouble ahead for the company.

Consistency of performance is the great brand builder. Inconsistency of performance is the great brand killer. When I open a Coke I don't hope it will taste the same as the last one. I know it will. If your company creates a standard of performance less than that, then you've got serious work to do, and you'd better do it fast.

You Figure It Out

The answer to anyone reading this who is still dissatisfied because I'm not giving them the specific "how-to" is this: Grow up. YOU figure it out. Very little of this stuff is advanced physics! Just pretend like you're back in school and your assignment is to figure it out and make it happen. Go. Scoot. Run along. You need to just figure it out!!!

In the early to mid-1980s, I did extensive marketing training for army officers whose new assignment was to head up a college ROTC program. The last day and a half of each one-week marketing seminar was an assignment in which eight officers were to work together to create a marketing plan using one of their campuses as the case study.

What always impressed me immensely was that if it had been a group of civilians, chances are very high that I would have had to answer questions about the assignment for an hour or two, clarifying and explaining exactly what to do. The beautiful thing about these army officers was that they listened to the assignment and went to work.

They figured it out.

Since that experience I've always had great respect for the leadership training of the U.S. Army. These men and women had a history of being given tough assignments without babying or hand-holding. They were used to stepping up to the assignment and getting results by using their own judgment and creativity. If only the rest of us were so mission oriented sometimes, business would be much simpler.

Just Do What You Think Will Work

I'm working with a company right now that is transitioning from a really terrible, creativity squashing culture into one in which people are trusted to use their heads and do the right thing. It's liberating for the employees and managers, although it's also a bit intimidating. For one thing, it's taken months for them to believe that the new leadership team is really serious about making things happen through the frontline people.

What's inspiring and fun to watch is that, when they truly comprehend that they are empowered, the employees are coming up with incredibly effective processes that create consistently outstanding performance. And it's happening, for lack of a better word, organically. The processes work because it's simply the best way to get results, not because of the enforcement of policies and rules.

Do it long enough, and it becomes part of the company DNA. It's how we do things here, and to do them differently would be like me, a left-hander, trying to write with my right hand. It wouldn't feel natural. That's how process works when it's done right. It happens naturally. Not because it's an enforced policy. It may begin as a measured, official way of doing things. But eventually the most effective processes become invisible, because they are just the way things are done. Ultimately, it's all about the culture—who we are and how we play the game.

Deciding in Advance

I've talked for years about the concept of making decisions in advance, an idea I got from my friend Phillip Van Hooser. Achieving outstanding performance on a consistent basis often comes down to simply that—we do what we do because the decision's been made in advance. We don't even have to think. We just act.

In my own business, I have a process by which minor expensing issues are settled with clients. My work almost always involves travel and I pride myself on keeping expenses as low as possible for the client. Once in a blue moon, though, a client will question, for example, plane fare. They might say that their travel department could have gotten a ticket for a few hundred dollars less.

In this situation, we go back to our process, which is to always let the client reimburse us whatever amount they feel is fair and appropriate. Over the years, we've probably absorbed a couple of thousand dollars in travel costs. And what did we gain? For starters, how about good will, a happy client, the reputation for being easy to work with, and less stress for everyone involved?

It's a process that works, and it doesn't have to be monitored or enforced anymore, because it's simply how we do it. The decision's been made in advance.

Simple—Not Easy

I don't mean to make any of this sound easy. And the bigger your organization, the tougher it is to achieve extraordinary performance on a consistent basis. But it is simple. It's not complicated.

You determine the behavior that you want, based on who you are, your vision, and your brand. Then you put a process in place to encourage that behavior on a regular basis, and supply the support system and environment to make it happen as easily and naturally as possible. Measure it, talk about it all the time, reward successes, and correct failures.

One day you look up and—voila! It's happening on its own. And you are one step closer to becoming indispensable.

15

Stop Apologizing— Start Doing Your Job

Measure Twice—Cut Once

We'd all do well to remember the old carpenter's saying of "measure twice, cut once" when it comes to creating consistency of performance. We're talking about the great brand builder here. Inconsistency of performance, on the other hand, is the great brand killer. If having a good experience with your company is a matter of how lucky I get in terms of which of your employees I encounter, then you've got a monster problem. The Driver of habitual dependency is the bedrock foundation on which becoming indispensable rests.

Suit Yourself

I got off my plane at the Springfield, Illinois, airport and headed for baggage claim. My hotel was near the airport, so I called them on the hotel display phone center and asked about the shuttle service. I needed to get to the hotel quickly, so I was fully prepared to take a taxi if the shuttle was going to be more than just a few minutes. No problem, I was assured by the hotel employee on the phone. The shuttle will be there in 10 minutes.

I go outside and wait at the shuttle pick-up area. Five minutes go by. Ten minutes go by. Fifteen minutes go by. I go back inside, call the hotel, and get the same employee on the phone. He says that the shuttle will be there in 10 minutes. I say that I can't wait any longer and will take a taxi. His reply was a sweet and simple, "Suit yourself."

A Pretty Good Shuttle Driver

When I arrived at the hotel I was, you might say, wound a bit tight. At the check-in desk, the clerk was the same guy I'd been talking to on the telephone. When I asked him why he had told me that the shuttle would be there in 10 minutes, when in fact the shuttle never even left the hotel, he responded with what was, for him, inescapable logic. "Sir, the shuttle driver has other things to do besides just drive the shuttle. He must have been busy."

As I proceeded to express my dissatisfaction in no uncertain terms, the other desk clerks kept their heads down and avoided any possible eye contact with me. I go to my room, shake it off, and chalk it up to another employee who doesn't care working for another company that doesn't care.

One of the other desk clerks must have told the manager what had happened, because about 15 minutes later I get a call from him. He said that he was very sorry, and that he was sending up a bottle of wine and a fruit plate as a gesture of apology. I thanked him and, as I hung up the phone thought to myself, "Now there's a manager who would make a pretty good shuttle driver."

Don't Apologize—Do Your Job

One sure sign of a second rate company is that there's a lot of apologizing going on. Everyone, from the phone operators to the sales staff to senior management seems to spend a great deal of time apologizing to customers for things that have gone wrong. If this is the case at your company, I'll say to you what I would say to that hotel manager. I don't want your apology. I want you to do your job!

Indispensable companies don't spend much time or effort on apologizing. They put that energy into training, building culture, and constant communication about what's important and what's expected. They understand that the ongoing investment in making sure that things get done right earns them a handsome return in customer satisfaction and loyalty.

Competence Trumps Nice

There are way too many companies out there that think that a stream of whining apologies will make it all better. We've all been through the "conflict resolution" and "handling customer complaints" courses that stress the importance of empathizing, listening, letting customers know you hear them and take them seriously, and, finally, offering a genuine apology. You know what? If I'm your customer I'd much rather you skip the customer complaint training and try a little more "do your job right the first time" training.

Of course, there are going to be situations where something falls through the cracks. People make mistakes. And of course you want to handle those situations in the most effective way possible. But let's get our priorities straight. We're back living in cliché-land again: "Funny how there's never enough time to do it right the first time, but always enough time to do it over."

Years ago, I bought a new car that had a handling problem. Whenever I got up to about 50 miles an hour, the car would start to shimmy, as if a wheel was out of balance or the car was out of alignment. I took it back to the service department where quite possibly the two nicest service managers in the world assured me that they'd take care of it immediately.

The next day I picked up the car, and as soon as I hit 50 miles an hour, there was the shimmy. Back to the auto dealer where the two shiny, nice service managers apologized profusely and assured me that they'd take care of the problem.

Rather than me write the preceding paragraph again, please just take a few moments to read it over and over about six times, because that's how many times I took the car back for this same problem. And each time the two happy, shiny, incredibly nice service managers would apologize and assure me they'd take care of the problem.

Only when I wrote the dealer and told him that I was going to contact the auto manufacturer's regional service representative did I begin to get any action. I think I might have also mentioned legal action. It turns out that the car had a defective wheel that was out of round. They replaced the wheel and solved the problem.

I wrote the dealer a follow-up letter and expressed my admiration for the two chippy, happy, shiny, incredibly nice and endlessly apologetic service managers. I also told him that they were incompetent and liars (I chose that word very carefully) and that, after this car, I would never do business with him again. I didn't want nice. I wanted the truth. I wanted my car fixed. I wanted them to do their jobs. Competence trumps nice every time.

Tell Me Exactly What Happened

Indispensable companies will be proactive in seeking out weaknesses in their performance before they become a pattern of problems. The worst companies avoid hearing customer complaints. The best companies sit their customers down and practically force them to tell them what to do better. Indispensable companies don't say, "Tell us what we're doing right." They say, "Tell us what we're doing wrong!" That kind of information is power.

My wife recently had a bad experience with a company, and she subsequently called their 1-800 customer complaint line. To be honest, she was expecting a cursory, cookie-cutter "we're sorry it happened and we hope we can continue to have you as a customer" kind of crapola that most companies spew out as a substitute for solving problems. To her pleasant surprise, what she got was something quite different.

The customer service representative asked Annette if she would be willing to take the time to explain, in great detail, exactly what had happened through the course of the entire experience. The rep listened carefully, and asked probing questions in response to everything that Annette told her. At the conclusion of the call, she told Annette exactly what action would be taken and how the situation would be followed up.

A few days later, Annette received a credit from the company, along with a formal letter of apology. It was nice. It was not what impressed her, however. What was impressive was the willingness, even the eagerness, of the company to find out exactly what had gone wrong, and then explain exactly what would be done to prevent the same thing from happening in the future. A complaining customer can be a gold mine of information if you are willing to get beyond issuing apologies as your standard response, and get down to the hard work of gaining information that you can use to get better.

The Lesson Is in Your Priorities

It's easy enough to see the lesson here and to remedy the problem of apologies versus performance. The lesson is in your priorities. Do an audit of what you spend your time doing and talking about in relation to customer complaints. First of all, how many complaints are you getting? If it's a regular topic of conversation around your company, and if you find yourself complaining about the amount of customer complaining that's going on, consider that a pretty clear signal that you're an organization in trouble.

If your priority seems to be handling complaints rather than doing what's necessary to prevent complaints, that's another signal that needs attention. If you're not already actively seeking feedback from customers to help identify patterns of poor performance, then it's time to begin. The key, of course, is follow-up. You must determine who's responsible, who's authorized, and who's empowered to see that the problem gets fixed, not on a case-by-case basis, but in a systematic way so that it doesn't happen again.

Indispensable companies look at one mistake as a potential if not real pattern of trouble and take a long view toward prevention. Mediocre companies look at one mistake as just that, one single isolated mistake. They put a band-aid on it, apologize to the customer, and then move on to patch up the next single isolated mistake.

It's Like Shoes

Relying on apologies as a way to handle performance issues is, to me, like buying cheap shoes. I can't afford cheap shoes. They wear out too quickly and have to be replaced way too often. A long time ago, I started buying the most expensive, highest quality shoes I could afford. I actually bought shoes that were, in the short term, more than I could afford. But they lasted. And they lasted and lasted and lasted.

If I see a problem that causes a customer complaint, I can either take the cheap shoes approach and go for the easiest quick fix available, or I can take the quality shoes approach and look for solutions that take more investment on the front end, but will serve me well for the long haul. Habitual dependability doesn't come cheap, but the payoff from the marketplace is immense.

16

Case Study: LawTalk

They Have to Buy It from Somebody

A few years ago, I became fascinated by, and ultimately a minor investor in, a company called LawTalk that seemed to have that dream-come-true market position: customers who have to buy their product. The catch, of course, is that the customers don't have to buy the product from LawTalk. There are plenty of competitors for the business.

The product is continuing education. Currently, 40 states have Minimum Continuing Legal Education (MCLE) requirements as a condition of maintaining a license to practice law. These states include approximately a million lawyers. Each lawyer is required to complete from 10 to 15 hours of MCLE per year. These lawyers have to buy this education from somebody. So far, so good.

How lucrative is this market? The North American market for MCLE programs and products is estimated to be over $2 billion annually. Additionally, there is a growing global MCLE marketplace, especially in the United Kingdom, Canada, and Australia/New Zealand. So you've got a big, fat, growing market for what LawTalk sells. Sweet.

It's precisely because of the sweetness of this market that other companies are hot and heavy into it, and vying for the same customers as LawTalk. So how does LawTalk become indispensable to its customers? They change the nature of what the customer is buying. By using the Drivers of creating a big picture outcome and constantly seeking to engage, enchant, and enthrall their customers, LawTalk has virtually become a category of one.

Making Continuing Education a Compelling Experience

For lawyers to retain their license, they have to go to school. The traditional approach has always been much what you might expect in a required learning credits environment. The model has generally been to provide lawyers with a traditional content directed school through which they can fulfill the learning requirements. For the customer it's often been a "Just let me sit through these 15 hours, get my requirement fulfilled, and let me out of here" situation.

LawTalk takes a highly customer-service focused, skills-oriented approach to the product, which has differentiated them and earned a remarkable degree of customer loyalty. They make going to school a compelling customer experience. Their programs and marketing efforts are based upon helping attorneys meet their MCLE hours while (1) learning skills they need to actively compete in the global marketplace; and (2) having a pleasant experience that is considerate of their schedules and budgets. It's the "pleasant experience" that is the hook.

Ever sat through a required seminar? Most of us have had to spend hours sitting through a seminar that our company required us to attend, or for continuing education credits, or for some other reason. It's usually not a pretty picture. LawTalk endeavors to change the very nature of the seminar experience so that what could be seen as a dreaded chore becomes an experience of choice. LawTalk's strategy is to make the customer's experience with them so useful, convenient, and pleasant that they will use LawTalk for their future MCLE needs, and will encourage them to recommend LawTalk to their colleagues.

From the LawTalk customer testimonial files, here are comments from three of their regular customers about the experience:

- "I dreaded sitting here for 12.5 hours, but the session was very entertaining and valuable. Thanks for a great day!"
- "Really good—way better than expected—far more interesting, rewarding, and FUN—than most CLE courses."
- "Kept me engaged and interested for 12 plus hours!!"

That's the key. That's the lesson. LawTalk looks beyond the product of providing a seminar to the Driver of big picture outcome to create a "great day" for the customer that was "interesting, rewarding, and FUN," and kept the customer "engaged."

The Highest Level of Customer Service—Ever

I interviewed LawTalk CEO John Dolan to find out how they go about becoming indispensable to customers.

Calloway: Bottom line this concept for me, John. How do you differentiate and lock-in customer loyalty?

Dolan: It's pretty simple—we are completely committed to providing the highest level of customer service that any lawyer has ever received at any continuing legal education seminar, EVER. The answer is always "Yes" when a lawyer calls and asks if we can help with continuing legal education requirements. We have done programs for as few as two lawyers, who desperately needed their requirement satisfied and had missed all previous opportunities from any suppliers including LawTalk.

Calloway: I know a lot of your differentiation comes from the experience you create around the seminars, but what about the core product itself, meaning the actual programs you put on? Is there anything in the content or presentation of the material that you feel acts as a differentiator for you?

Dolan: The actual presenters at our seminars are definitely a "value added" for our customers. When they see our presenters, who are all professional speakers first and lawyers second, they rave because most lawyers have never seen a truly professional speaker who also happens to be a lawyer. Instead, they are used to legal experts who do not speak very well.

Calloway: What about the very nature of the seminar experience? It seems there's only so much you can do to make it pleasant or compelling.

Dolan: We "concierge" our seminars. That is, we provide almost any service that any lawyer requests, whether it's help with hotel reservations, help with travel, dinner reservations, or something technical like assistance with multiple state admission compliance.

Calloway: One of the Drivers in becoming indispensable is to engage, enchant, and enthrall. How do you do that?

Dolan: My wife and partner Irene Garcia Dolan, who is president of LawTalk, is a gracious hostess who is always looking for a way to provide the extras, from little details like candy on all the tables to cassette or CD players for the lawyers who need to listen to the self-study materials when we are not in session so they can meet an impending deadline. Irene even invites attendees' spouses to dine with us and, speaking of dining, we provide all meals and refreshments. Meals and refreshments are almost never provided at continuing legal education programs. Lawyers are almost always "on their own."

Calloway: An important factor in locking in customer loyalty is the Driver of continuous connection. How does this play a part with LawTalk's customer retention?

Dolan: The big things include keeping in contact, offering free monthly web-based continuing legal education, keeping our customers informed about continuing legal education requirements, and providing an extensive web site full of resource information available to our customers. But the big things are not as significant as some of the "little things." Little things like remembering our customers' names when we see them at the registration table, recognizing the oldest State Bar member and the newest State Bar member at every seminar, and providing little gifts, specially chosen for our returning customers.

Calloway: So does the continuous connection ultimately come down to personal relationships in a business that is generally considered rather impersonal in nature?

Dolan: Obviously, from the way I've described our approach to this business, you can see that we are committed to personal relationships with our customers. Lawyers don't get this very often.

A Transferable Strategy

I simply can't think of a business or product with which this same basic strategy wouldn't work. Wrap your core product offering with an experience that will engage, enchant, and enthrall the customer with the goal of producing a big picture outcome that compels loyalty, referrals, and repeat business. Even if you don't have direct personal contact with your buyer, at some point something is delivered to them in some way. That moment of delivery of the product is your chance to become indispensable. Whether it's the ease of ordering from your web site, the way the product is packaged, or how you interact with customers when they phone you, the opportunity is there.

17

The Customer Decides

Stories from the Front Lines

My only direct experience in retail was in high school, when I worked in a men's clothing store during the holidays. Other than that, I've always been a business-to-business (B2B) guy. My customers tend to be big corporations. What I know is true in my B2B arena, however, is that retail consumer behavior moves up the food chain. That corporate or industrial buyer that you deal with is also a consumer. Once she has an experience on the retail level that delights her, she's going to expect the same thing from you. Or at least your version of it. Claiming that it's not fair to expect the same kind of service from you as she expects from her corner market won't cut you any slack. She won't care.

What follows are stories from the front lines. All of these stories are about street smarts. The street is where buying behavior trends are born. They then travel from retail up the food chain to influence the buying factors in corporate purchasing. Once that industrial purchasing agent buys a book on Barnes & Noble.com, or has an extraordinary experience in a local steakhouse, it influences her buying behavior back at work.

These are testimonies from people, in their own words, about businesses that they find indispensable. Here's the law of the marketplace: How well we think we're doing doesn't matter. It only matters how well the customer thinks we're doing. What we're after here are lessons that will get us a win with the customer. The point is to look at what works in a market different from yours, in order to be ahead of the curve when your customers start to want the same thing. If you're tempted to skip this chapter because you think these ideas don't apply to your customers, do so at your own risk. Retail behavior always moves across industry lines and up the buying food chain.

Not Easy

Brian Palmer is not an easy guy to impress. I asked him to submit an example of a business that he found to be extraordinary or that had demonstrated remarkable performance in a way that had clearly differentiated it from the rest. After a few days, Brian wrote me to say that he was stumped. He simply hadn't run across that level of performance. Did I mention that Brian Palmer is not easily impressed?

The Beer Guy

Then, about a week later, I received the following e-mail from Brian:

> It was a last minute thing. A friend gave me tickets to the Chicago White Sox–Detroit Tiger game. My eleven-year-old son is mad for sports and, in particular, attending

sporting events. With baseball mitt poised on hand, Adam eagerly followed the game and especially all foul balls.

Though I was not patronizing the beer vendors that evening, one of them noticed Adam's eagerness and encouraged and inquired each time he went by. In the ninth inning, he once again asked if Adam had been successful. When told no, he reached into his tray of beer cans and pulled out a ball noting, "I got this for you from Ozzie." Ozzie Guillen is the White Sox Manager.

Four Fundamental Lessons

The White Sox should make the Beer Guy their director of marketing. Who knows? Maybe he is. This guy used four fundamental principles of winning and keeping customers to knock the socks off my hard-to-impress friend. This is just another example in a never-ending stream that convinces me that the core challenge in business, which is the challenge of winning and keeping customers, comes down to a few basic ideas that can be adapted to virtually any market arena.

Duh: Identify Customer Need

Brian wrote, "Though I was not patronizing the beer vendors that evening, one of them noticed Adam's eagerness and encouraged and inquired each time he went by." This is straight out of Sales 101. Find out what your customer's buying. Pay attention. Watch for clues. And keep a particular lookout for emotional clues. Adam's eagerness and that baseball glove on his hand are obvious clues that there's an emotional need here looking to be filled.

The failure of most people in the Beer Guy's position would have been that with Brian not buying any beer, they would have stopped looking for clues as to what else was going on. Old saying: When all you have is a hammer then all you see is nails. When I'm talking to a prospective client, I go into consultant mode as if he had already hired me to help him find the right vendor to solve his problem. It ultimately may or may not be me. But I'm not trying to talk him into buying what I've got. I'm trying to help him find the right solution. It's a long-term, big picture strategy. Brian's Beer Guy was looking beyond selling a beer.

See the Big Picture Outcome

Remember that Brian wasn't even buying any beers from this guy. And yet, as Brian wrote, "In the ninth inning, he once again asked if Adam had been successful. When told no, he reached into his tray of beer cans and pulled out a ball noting, 'I got this for you from Ozzie.' " So what prompted this guy to get a baseball for a kid whose dad wasn't even buying one beer, for crying out loud? Big picture outcome. Give me a company full of employees who all see the big picture outcome, and I'll run the competition out of town. This guy was selling the White Sox as a great experience. He was able to look past the small picture, transactional perspective of selling beer to a big picture perspective of selling the company. How much more competitive would your company be if everyone there was selling the experience to every customer every time?

Engage, Enchant, and Enthrall

Note that the Beer Guy didn't just say, "Here, kid. Here's a baseball." That would have been a nice thing to do, but wouldn't have packed near the marketing punch as saying, "I got this for you from Ozzie." Do you see the impact of his gesture just sky-rocket by making it personal, from Ozzie to the Beer Guy to Adam? That makes it magic. That's precisely why I advise my clients against counting on getting very much return on the use of such marketing tools as "generic newsletters" that are written for anybody and just insert the sending company or individual's name at the end. Give me the same thing you give to everybody, and it may have some positive impact. But treat me special, or in a way that I perceive as being special, and you are one step closer to becoming indispensable.

Give Away Some Baseballs

This one comes up again and again: Give it away. If what you bring to market is good stuff, then give it away. Let go of some money and give free samples. If your product is junk, then, of course, this "give it away" strategy won't work. But if you believe in your product or service, then give it away, and people will want more. For the cost of one baseball, the White Sox have not only captured the attention of hard to impress Brian Palmer, but they've also captured the imagination, and possibly the lifelong loyalty, of Mr. Adam Palmer, age 11. Can you say "income stream?"

The Follicle God

Suze Baez of Belmont Shore, California, offers Robert, her hairdresser, as her choice for what's indispensable in her life. Here's her story:

> I have never had a hair stylist who I am more loyal to than the follicle god who works on me now. I am so loyal to this

man that, when he had a family emergency and was over-
seas for over a month and a half, I walked around with roots
showing, and that isn't something that I have ever done
with a previous hairdresser. Delilah thought Samson had
hair issues; I make Samson look like he is low maintenance.

Lesson: Create loyalty so that when you or your product isn't
available, your customer will go without rather than turn to
a competitor.

I was introduced to Robert (my hairdresser) through my
neighbor after I had managed to turn my hair an interesting orangey-gun metal color. God bless him, he could have
made me feel like the cheap doofus that I was for attempt-
ing to do my own hair, but he went out of his way to make
sure that I was comfortable, listening attentively to what "I
thought" I wanted. He patiently placated me and looked
through pictures of what my hair had previously looked
like and then assured me that he would make me look gorgeous again. Anybody that tells me I am gorgeous or that I
have the capacity to look gorgeous, well he just scored
points right there. Flattery will get you everywhere.

Lesson: Never make your customer feel like a cheap doofus,
even if he is. You're in the business of solving problems for
customers, not expecting them to know as much as you about
what you do.

Even though he is a one-man operation, he runs the most
efficient business I have ever experienced in that industry.
I have spent hundreds of dollars going to a Beverly Hills
hair artist, with several assistants running around waiting
on the stylist and me hand and foot, and I still get a better

cut and experience from Robert. When I am in his chair, he has the ability to make me feel like his entire attention is on me and me alone.

Lesson: When you are my customer, you are the single most important person in the world to me.

He must keep a card of our conversations in a little file somewhere, or he has the memory of an elephant. He always remembers the last things we talked about, from my mother's health to the latest business dealings that I had discussed previously. He is a smooth reader of mine and other peoples' moods and seems to intuitively know when to speak and when to just let you be in your own little world. And, the most amazing thing about him is that he has the ability to say, "No, that won't work for you," without me realizing that he said, "no" . . . and, I still walk out happy with what he has done with my hair.

Lesson: Just as "all politics are local," it's equally true that "all business is personal." Your customer may be a buyer for a multinational corporation. Believe me, it's personal.

I knew that I was going to be a customer for life when after my first color and cut from him, he called me the next day at my office to check and make sure that I liked the color and cut. And that if anything needed to be adjusted to my satisfaction, I could come back in at no charge until I was happy with the finished product. I have never had a hairdresser make that offer and he truly meant it.

After one of my appointments with him, I just didn't like the way my hair was styling when I tried to do it on my own. He made his next day call as usual and I told him it wasn't doing what I wanted it to do. He squeezed me in that afternoon and managed to make "the hair that has a mind of its' own" do exactly what I wanted it to do . . . at no extra charge.

I have referred Robert to several family members and friends; everyone says the same thing, "I love him! I hope to God he never retires!"

Lesson: If the customer's not happy, make it right. Even if it costs you money to do so, make it right. It's the difference between making money on a one-time transaction and making a fortune on a lifetime stream of income.

Lemons to Lemonade

Mark Sanborn is the author of the best-selling book *The Fred Factor.* Mark knows more than a thing or two about business, and he's no pushover when it comes to having his own expectations as a customer met. Mark had a bad experience with an insurance broker that one employee was able to not only salvage, but turn into a satisfied customer scenario. Here's his story:

A few years ago I had a problem with my insurance broker. I appealed to the owner of the agency and got no satisfaction. He handled the situation very poorly. I decided I would not do any new business with the agency in the future.

Of course, they were my agency of record for a number of existing policies. Several months later I had a question around one of those policies and was chagrinned that I had to call these folks to get an answer. When I made the call, I was routed to a woman named Theresa. I began by saying, "Your records may or may not reflect the really bad service I've received from you in the past. I would prefer to never have to talk with anyone at your agency again, but unfortunately you have information I need. Here's my question. . . ." I wasn't mean, but my words were direct. Theresa quickly got me the answer I needed. But before we hung up, she said, and I paraphrase, "Mr. Sanborn, I don't know all that happened to make you feel the way you do about this agency. But I promise you this: I will personally handle your account in the future and do everything I can to provide you the service you deserve."

In the process, a woman I had only met by phone (and not under ideal circumstances) regained my loyalty. Yep, I'm still using that agency today.

Lesson: Here's one that is as scary a cautionary tale as it is a story with a happy ending. If the boss has to count on his employees to clean up his messes, then he should fire himself. This situation also gets to the issue of consistency of performance. While Theresa has earned Mark's customer loyalty, any business that operates under the principle of "depends on who you get" is heading for trouble. This company got lucky that Theresa was able to pull the situation out of the fire, but in the long haul, they'd better have an agency full of Theresa-like employees if they want to survive, much less compete and win.

What's the Deal with Dry Cleaners?

I think that graduate schools of business are missing the boat by focusing on companies like Harley Davidson, Starbucks, and Southwest Airlines for their case studies in how to win and keep customers. Whenever I ask an audience to name their favorite companies, I always get a huge number of dry cleaners given as examples of extraordinary service and the ensuing customer loyalty. Conversely, nothing seems to raise the ire of today's consumer more than a dry cleaner that misses the mark.

Because I hear so much feedback about dry cleaners from people who have sworn their allegiance to their own favorite, I am convinced that if I could run my consulting business according to the same principles as these guys, I would be wildly successful. And it's true. All of the lessons are pretty easily transferable from a dry cleaner to any other business. The trick, as always, is to see beyond the differences and look toward figuring out what's your version of what they do.

What follows are the stories of three very happy customers of three remarkable dry cleaners. Remember the point, which is to see what lessons in becoming Indispensable are to be found that have application to any business in any market arena. Here are the stories, along with a look at the lessons to be learned that can benefit any business.

The Magic Touch

Joy Baldridge absolutely loves her dry cleaners, Magic Touch Cleaners in Stamford, Connecticut. Here is her story:

> Robert, the owner, is from Haiti. One day I asked if Robert could help me with my French, by speaking only in French to me whenever I came in. He said, "Mais bien sur!" (But of course!)
>
> *Lesson:* If your customers want to do business in a particular way, and it doesn't disrupt your ability to do what you do, let them make up the rules.
>
> Over the past several years, we have spoken solely in French to the point where my two-year-old, Mackenzie, even says

an enthusiastic, "Bonjour!" whenever we drive by or stop in. She also knows "Comma ca va?" and "Ca va bien!" Robert is very supportive and reassuring when I struggle to find a word in French from my seventh grade class over 30 years ago.

Robert also has a big wicker basket of small candies on the counter in his shop from which my kids and I request certain favorites. My eight-year-old, Wilson, and I are particularly fond of the banana Laffy Taffy, Smarties, and cherry Jolly Ranchers. Sometimes when I go to Magic Touch before picking up Wilson from school, I pick out a few of his favorite candies, and when he gets in the car I give a pop quiz and ask him to guess where I just was. He always knows it was the dry cleaners.

Lessons: People are absolute suckers for anything you do for his kids. If you can make your business kid-friendly, the parents will love you for it. I'm in a strictly business-to-business marketplace, but anytime I ask a client about his kids, I score points. When I can ask that CEO in Arlington Heights, Illinois, how his son's hockey team is doing, it's nothing except smart business, in addition to just being a nice way to deal with people. Sincerity. The old joke about faking it notwithstanding, the truth is that you can't fake it. You're either interested in people or you're not. If you are, it helps.

My take is, yeah, Magic Touch cleans clothes well, but they also are friendly, responsive, and give free French lessons and sweet treats. Despite it being a supposed chore on the personal to-do list, I feel good going there, and I feel better coming out. What a great thing! My favorite businesses are those in which the people are really, really good at what they do and are willing to have fun, too!

Lesson: Are you fun to do business with? I don't care what you're selling, if you can become the best part of your customer's day, you win. Stay competitive with product, price, quality, and service, and differentiate by simply being more fun to do business with. One computer consulting firm client of mine makes "being thoroughly delightful" a performance requirement for its employees. This isn't for the sake of being precious. This is a well-thought-out, bottom-line, strategic decision that management feels is their ace in the hole in earning customer loyalty.

It Takes a Village

Here's the story of dry cleaner indispensability as told by Hunter McCarty, who is the embodiment of what every business wants—a customer for life:

> For several years, I had used a dry cleaner that was locally owned and provided personal service. The dry cleaner was sold to a larger company and the name changed. Although the company changed hands, I decided to continue to use their service. Shortly after I made this decision, I noticed that they did not take the same interest in the processing of my cleaning nor did the new regime know who I was as a customer. The crowning blow came when they broke some buttons on my collar and then replaced them with buttons that were larger than the original buttons and would not fit the buttonholes.

Lesson: When there's an ownership or management change, the new sheriff in town would be well served to do a little initial customer research and find out what has worked up to now. If you're going to change the way things are done, at least give customers a heads up that change is on the way.

For a couple of years I had received a Christmas card from a competitive cleaner with a discount coupon, and I decided to try them out since I could be no worse off. The name of the new cleaners was Village Cleaners, and they were convenient and on my way to work.

Lesson: When I began my business the single most successful marketing tool I used was post cards. I used them in order to be everywhere, all the time. I didn't know when a prospective client might be in that decision-making mode, so I had to try and be, if not top of mind, at least somewhere around the edges of his mind when that decision was made. Be where your potential customers are. In this case, the Christmas card, year after year, paid off.

I began using them, and I liked the fact that they were locally owned and operated. The employees grew to know me by name, and soon they were definitely providing what I would call personalized service. They always made it a point to respond to me when I came to the establishment. In fact, they have gotten so good that as I drive into the parking lot, they immediately pull my order and have it waiting on the hanger when I walk into the store. They make every effort to provide the type of personalized service that I had come to expect, and they do go out of their way to make sure that I am pleased. Have they ever broken a button? Sure, but they replaced it with the correct size. Would I ever consider leaving them? No way!

Lesson: Know the customer. Know what the customer wants. Give it to him. Continue to ask if you're meeting the customer's needs. Never make assumptions about customer satisfaction.

I Pay Extra

For those of you who, like me, have absolutely no interest in competing on price, there is a lot to learn from the story of Glenna Salsbury and her devotion to The French Cleaners. For this business, it's all about making it personal. Here's Glenna's story:

> I pay extra to have my clothes cleaned—happily. That's because of Maryse Mimric. Maryse and her husband Guy own The French Cleaners in Scottsdale, Arizona. Maryse loves my style in clothes! She remembers which pieces are mine without looking at the ticket. Maryse also likes my choice in perfume. She tells me she likes cleaning and pressing my clothes because she can smell my perfume as she presses. Maryse sometimes posts my picture on her bulletin board as a "happy customer." Maryse took the picture herself and had me autograph it.
>
> *Lesson:* We've all heard that "the customer is always right." Add the following: Your customer is cool. Your customer is hip. Your customer smells good. Your customer rocks. Repeat after me—Honor thy customer.

Comfort Food

Shifting gears away from dry cleaners, Diane Sparks is captured by the habitual dependability of, believe it or not, french fries! Here's her story.

> I've really thought through this, and I kept coming up with places that I would not go back to (ha! ha!). Funny how easy it is to focus on the negative. Then I had a particularly stressful day at work, and all I could think about was go to McDonald's and order some french fries! I absolutely love

McDonald's french fries! They make me feel safe! So I thought about this.

I have loved McDonald's french fries since I was five years old. The McDonald's opened in Baton Rouge, Louisiana, in 1964. My Dad will tell you to this day that all I ever wanted to eat was McDonald's french fries. In 40 years, their fries have never changed. Why change perfection?

I have come to rely on their consistency. They've been consistent no matter where I have lived or traveled. As crazy as this sounds, there is a safe, home feeling for me when I eat McDonald's french fries.

Lesson: Get it right every time for 40 years.

Cheap Joe's

Camille Engel is a renowned artist who had a rather remarkable experience with an art supply house. Here's her story:

> I ordered some painting supplies from cheapjoes.com (Cheap Joe's art supplies). When the tornadoes damaged our area last spring, Cheap Joe's mailed me and all their area artists a postcard that said that if we lost our art supplies due to the tornadoes, Cheap Joe's would like to help replace them. I was so impressed with that offer, I remembered it months later and shared it in art class along with other students who ordered from Cheap Joe's. We all became very loyal to Cheap Joe's.

> *Lesson:* When you're in trouble, you remember who was there to offer help. Cheap Joe may be a lot of things, but he's not cheap. The company's willingness to come to the aid of a community of artists made an impression, and it resulted in long-term customer loyalty. When the going gets tough for your customers, be there.

They Answer Their Phone

You'll win customer Eileen McDargh's heart, loyalty, and money if you just answer your phone. Here's her story:

> I had my digital Canon Elf stolen at a convention. It's my second Canon. Bill (Eileen's husband) is trying to get me to spend less money on another brand for a replacement. I want my Canon . . . why? They answer their phone. They have great, and live—real-time and real-person tech help for FREE. What a novel approach. I told him I'd spend money for Canon because, they'll be here for me!
>
> *Lesson:* Be there when the customer needs your help. The customer will be there when you need her money.

Twenty-Four Years Later

When I read the indispensable story from CoraMarie Clark of Calgary, Canada, I was tempted to just submit it to the publisher as the entire book. I wanted to say, "Read this. Any questions?" I ultimately decided to add a bit more to the book, but I offer you this story as just about the ultimate lesson in what becoming indispensable looks like from a customer's point of view:

> My most memorable experience as a customer began 24 years ago, around the time my first child was born, with the purchase of a very expensive set of waterless cookware and knives from a door-to-door salesman.
>
> As you can imagine, 24 years later, the cookware and knives show a bit of wear and tear. Recently, a handle broke off one of the pots. That, along with a dent and small chip on another pot, a few rust spots on one knife, and the tip broken off another knife, had me feeling annoyed. The

cookware had a lifetime warranty, but when I divorced, I had not saved any documentation proving that I was the owner or that my cookware carried a lifetime warranty.

After finding a telephone number for Royal Prestige on the Web, I was delighted with the incredibly helpful Royal Prestige employee, Tracey, who answered the phone. I told Tracey the approximate time I had purchased the cookware and what my surname had been at the time of purchase as well as informed her that I had no Warranty papers.

Seconds later, Tracey asked if I had lived on Glenhill Drive in Cochrane, Alberta, when the cookware was purchased. She had accessed my entire file, even though the purchase had been made in a precomputer time.

I felt Tracey totally heard and validated everything I told her. She promptly assured me that replacements would be sent as soon as they received my damaged cookware and knives in the mail. I was thrilled—and very much looking forward to the arrival of the new pieces.

Two weeks later, Noelle, another Royal Prestige employee, phoned to tell me that she was in the process of packaging my replacement items. She had just realized that I would probably not be very happy when my new knives arrived, as Royal Prestige had recently upgraded the knives they were selling, so my new knives would not match the remaining pieces of my original set. I immediately wondered how much she was going to try to charge me to upgrade the rest of my knives. What she actually asked me is: "Would you mind if Royal Prestige sends you a complimentary entire new set of knives? It's very important to us that our customers are totally happy with our products!" Not only was I happy, I was ELATED!!

Lesson: Any questions?

Index